TALES OF GODS
IN HINDU
MYTHOLOGY

TALES OF GODS
IN HINDU
MYTHOLOGY

V. SATISH

PARTRIDGE

A Penguin Random House Company

To order additional copies of this book, contact
Toll Free 800 101 2657 (Singapore)
Toll Free 1 800 81 7340 (Malaysia)
orders.singapore@partridgepublishing.com

www.partridgepublishing.com/singapore

CONTENTS

To Lord Vinayaka; Remover of obstacles and the great
god of success. You are the seat of knowledge. You
are the son of Lord Shiva. This book is written
because of your grace that you shower upon me.

It was you that made the world to realise the importance
of parents when you circulated them and
took away the fruit of knowledge.

It was you that gave the priority to wisdom when you saved the
great epic, Mahabharata from ruination when you
broke your tusk and wrote on the palm leaf.

I offer my respectful obeisance to you before
attempting to write this book.

To my parents; Vengadasalam and Dhanaletchumee
who had supported me all this while.

To my brothers; Navine Nalechami and Kehshen Kumar
who pushed me through in times of trouble.

To my eternal friends; Deepaa Selvaraja, Kavemallar
Tharmaraja and Neshaa Punusamy

To Santhini Perumal and Shalini Perumal; both
of you motivated me in times of turbulence.

To Preamini Satiavanan and Yogadharshimy
Peter; who are enthusiastic about my book.

PREFACE

In this modern world, the knowledge about gods especially Hindu gods are disappearing over the years.

Lord Shiva said 'On a cloudy day, to the common man's eyes the sun seemed to be covered. But the fact is because the sunshine creates the cloud, the sun can never actually be covered, even though the whole sky may be cloudy. Similarly, less intelligent men claim there is no god' (***Lord Shiva to Lord Krishna; KRSNA –SUPREME PERSONALITY OF GODHEAD***).

Keeping these things in mind, I had attempted to introduce some of Hindu most prominent gods to the world by presenting their stories. Through these magical tales, one may understand few things about these gods.

The historians and anthropologists cannot supply the evidence of events that happened beyond 40 000 years ago. However the Hindu Vedic literatures such as the Vedas and the Puranas provide us with magical account of gods extending billions of years to the past.

This book '**Tales About Gods in Hindu Mythology**' is a fluid summary of the gods pastimes. I have modified the stories for the enjoyment of the readers rather than mundane reading of the narration of these tales. Besides, I have included in some tales regarding the historical events that took place and even some extra information regarding these stories. The purpose is to provide some information besides enjoying the stories.

INTRODUCTION

Since time dawns, we; humans are fascinated about gods. The questions that we ask ourselves are usually Who are these beings?

Gods were nothing but the primeval force that governs the affairs of the universe. The letter G in God means generator, O means operator and D means destroyer. The cosmic manifestation is undergoing these processes over and over again without us realising it.

Hinduism has 33 million gods or sometimes known as demigods. The leader of them is King Indra. He is the lord of thunderclouds and king of the heavenly planets. Above Indra are the Trinity of Gods; namely Lord Brahma (creator), Lord Vishnu (preserver), Lord Shiva (destroyer). Below Indra, are the lesser gods like Yama (god of death) and Varuna (god of seas and waters).

The stories of various gods had been carefully recorded in ancient vedic literatures such as the *Vedas, Puranas* and *Isopanisad*. To support these stories, there is the *Bhagavad- Gita*. The *Bhagavad-Gita* is the actual science of God and the essence of the *Vedas* itself.

In this modern age of Kali, people are not interested anymore with gods. This is the influence of this Dark Age. When people are not interested with spirituality and self realization can never be able to control their senses. Thus, they are actually killing themselves slowly and the time is up for them to die, they will be forced to take birth as lower animals or hellish beings. Thus one must take into account hearing the tales of gods

THE BIRTH OF LORD BRAHMA AND THE CREATION OF THE UNIVERSE

At the beginning of time, there was nothing. There were no planets and stars. The universe itself has not existed in this time. It is just darkness.

However in the darkness, only the God of the name Sri Vishnu existed. It is explained by Bhaktivedanta Swami that Lord Vishnu lies on the causal ocean known as the Garbodhaka. The ocean itself was formed from the dissolution of the planetary systems.

Bhaktivedanta Swami described about this ocean in the book entitled Krsna. It is said that that the ocean is the origin of material creation. From the word Karana came the Malay word; 'kerana'. It means reason. Thus the Karana Ocean is also known as the Ocean of Reason for this ocean is the ultimate reason of creation of this world.

The proof of before the existence of universe and the gods, Lord Vishnu existed is explained in the *Brahma-Samhita* and the *Vedas*. At this moment, Lord Vishnu is so gigantic, and here He is known as Maha Vishnu.

It is because of Maha Vishnu, the creation begins to take place. Maha-Vishnu threw His glance to the bubbling water of the Karana Ocean or the Garbodhaka Ocean. In this way, the Supreme Lord injected His male energy into the waters of Karana Ocean. Immediately, the bubbles began to emanate from His body. Each bubble is actually one universe. Thus, the concept of multiple universes or parallel universe put forward by modern scientist is a fact as immure able bubbles that emanate from His gigantic body are universes. This is the ultimate beginning of creation that occurs before creation of gods.

Maha-Vishnu expanded Himself into many uncountable forms, which are much smaller than Himself. These expansions are known as the Garbodaksayayi Vishnu.

Garbodaksayayi Vishnu entered into each and every bubble which is actually a particular universe. When Garbodaksayayi Vishnu entered these universes, His other expansion known as Ananta Sesa also entered into each bubble.

The tale of Brahma's creation actually takes place in this particular universe, which is a bubble to the great Maha Vishnu. It is said that in each universe there is a Brahma, and we do not have the knowledge of how the Brahmas' of the other universes look like.

Lord Vishnu was lying comfortably and meditating in His sleeping posture on His snake-bed of the name Ananta-Sesa. This sleeping posture is known as *yoga-nindram*. Ananta Sesa is a multi-hooded snake which was floating on the great ocean of milk in the planet known as Vaikuntha.

Upon meditation, a long cord started to emerge from Lord Vishnu's deep navel and subsequently began to move upwards defying the planet's gravitational pull.

The umbilical cord began to journey away from Lord Vishnu's navel further and further upwards until it penetrated the atmosphere of the planet Vaikuntha. Not stopping there, the cord shot upwards beyond and beyond into darkness.

Finally the cord stopped moving all of a sudden. At the end of the cord, there was a pink lotus flower which is still in the bud stage. The lotus petals closed tightly but some sort of effulgence shone from the flower. All of a sudden, the petals began to open and a man was sitting in the lotus flower with his eyes closed tightly.

The man has four heads, with each head facing the four cardinal points of the world, namely north, south, east and west. Each head was wearing a golden helmet bedecked with jewels. Four hands emerge from the man's body and each hand was found to be holding different things namely a prayer book, a blooming lotus flower, prayer beads and a water pot. His body was nicely constructed and decorated with various jewellery and ornaments. On the forehead of each head was painted with an auspicious clay marking known as *tilaka*. Each face was handsome with raised nose, thick eyebrows and rosy lips. This man is none other than the Hindu god of creation known as Brahma.

It is confirmed in various Vedic literatures that Lord Brahma is the first created being from the navel of Garbodhakasayi Vishnu. The *gopis* (eternal girlfriends of Lord Krishna) stated that, 'From Your navel emanated the original lotus flower which is the birth site of Brahma; the creator.'

Brahma opened his eyes which are eight in number and looked around without turning his heads as he doesn't have to. He saw nothing but darkness in the four directions. Brahma tried to find other lives and subsequently tilted his head and peered down. He saw that a long cord that connects the lotus flower which he was sitting. Lord Brahma stood and levitated. Now He has a greater view and saw that the cord goes deeper and deeper into an unknown planet. (Brahma did not know that the planet is Vaikuntha).

"Where this cord goes?" asked the god of creation to himself. Feeling very curious, Brahma descended from the lotus flower and made way to the planet. He wanted to know the source of the cord which was his birthplace. Ultimately, Lord Brahma entered into the planet and a vast ocean greeted his eyes. The waves of the ocean roared when Brahma came nearer to its surface. However the cord goes deeper into the ocean. "What a long cord is it, well I shall not give up in finding the source", said Brahma to himself surprised. The Lord without any hesitation dived into the ocean. The ocean rippled once Brahma dived into it.

Lord Brahma swam and eventually he came to the ocean bed and within the ocean, Brahma saw a super-large palace within the ocean.

"This palace is so big! Who is here must be the one who created me, I must find my creator", said Brahma with a determinant aim.

The palace was decorated with billions and billions of pillars. The pillars itself were decorated with jewels. The glaring effulgence of these jewels made Brahma perplexed.

Eventually Brahma came to the main quarters of the palace. At the main quarters He saw a gigantic serpent with millions of hoods. Each hood was decorated with jewels beautifully dazzling. Each hood has two eyes which appeared to be very fearful. The body was so white like snow and the necks were bluish. The serpent known as Ananta-Sesa or Ananta-Deva. On the body of Ananta-Sesa which was decorated with pillows, Sri Vishnu was lying very comfortably. His skin is just dark blue just like the colour of clouds in the rainy season. He wore a yellow garment and held a disc which is razor sharp (*Sudharshana cakra*), a lotus flower, a conch shell (*Pancajanya*) and a large club (*Kaumodaki*) was lying beside the Lord

Lord Brahma stood like a statue for a while in front of Sri Vishnu, surprised and as well as scared seeing the gigantic form of the Lord. But this moment of surprise and fear doesn't last long because as if told by someone, Lord Brahma sank to one knee upon Lord Vishnu. This action of Brahma was significant because he understood that he came from Vishnu. In other words, Brahma knew that Lord Vishnu is his father. In Hindu culture, a son or daughter must pay respects to their parents when they see their parents. This is shown by Lord Brahma respecting his great father.

Lord Brahma says, "My Lord, the material creation is created because of You as Maha Vishnu glances upon the womb of this material nature. Just as a male injects his sperm into the womb of a female that results in formation of foetus and subsequently an individual, similarly You creates this material nature by transferring Your energy to the womb of material nature."

This is confirmed by the statement in *Brahma-Samhita* that 'Lord Vishnu is lying in the Karana Ocean. When He exhales, innumerable universes come into existence and when He inhales, these universes enter within Him. Bhaktivedanta Swami explained this is how the material creation is created and destroyed in a cyclic pattern. Actually, the concept of ultimate destruction does not appear in Hinduism, as the universes is created and destroyed and re- created.

Lord Brahma paused for a while and continued, "My Lord, it is You that expands from Maha-Vishnu into Garbodhakasayi Vishnu and I have not the slightest idea of what are you are going to do after this. I have not known my purpose yet. Why You created me from Your navel? But I believe that You will reveal to me the reason."

Brahma said further, "Lord Govinda, please therefore disclose the purpose of my birth."

Upon hearing His son's prayers and respects, Lord Vishnu opened his lotus like eyes, smiled and woke up from His lying position and sat. Ananta whimpered suddenly.

Lord Vishnu said, "My dear Brahma, what you said is true and I accept it without any hesitation. Thus, now it is your duty to satisfy me as I created you in order to create the universe and organisms in it." He paused a while.

"You may create other gods to help you in these affairs. However, you must meditate for thousand years and after the meditation, you will receive the knowledge from Me to create." explained Lord Vishnu furthur.

"I will carry out Your wish immediately", replied Brahma solemnly, rising. He bowed to Lord Vishnu with great respect; Lord Vishnu extends His right hand, blessing His son.

Lord Brahma stormed out of the palace and swam to the surface where he reached the cord which is still up in the air. Lord Brahma flew upwards and reached His lotus flower. He sat there and started to meditate. Brahma meditated for one thousand years according to gods calculations. Later at the end of his meditation, Brahma received knowledge from Lord Vishnu regarding the method of creation.

This knowledge of creation is analogous to some permission by the Lord. We must understand that knowledge is never ours to own. That means we are not the master of the knowledge. Everything comes from Vishnu. For example, in this particular case of Brahma to create, it is not possible for Brahma to immediately create the universe as soon as he opens his eyes. He requires his father's knowledge. It is not his knowledge but is Vishnu's. Similarly, what we learnt is never ours and never will be. The original knowledge comes from Vishnu and is passed down and distributed among the beings in this universe. Thus we can conclude the proprietor of knowledge is none other than Vishnu, as He is the original Supreme Personality of Godhead. It is said that Lord Vishnu is wearing knowledge in the form of necklace. Just as a necklace is unimportant for an individual in general, similarly Lord Vishnu's knowledge is so vast and is unlimited, so even knowledge itself has no importance to Him.

Lord Brahma thus created the universe, namely planets and stars. However he has not created any beings yet. Brahma meditated a while closing his eyes and suddenly a baby sprang out from his mind. The baby floated in the space. Without any prior information or warning, another three babies sprang out of Brahma's mind. These are the quartet brothers. The four brothers were called as the 'Four Kumaras'. The Four Kumaras were namely Sanaka, Sananta, Sanandana and Sanat-kumara.

The four Kumaras were the first sons born out of Brahma. They appeared like small children but their body gives off effulgence. They wore no clothes except for a piece of white linen cloth covering their pubic area.

Lord Brahma addressed them, "My dear Kumaras, I created you from my mind so that all of you can carry out my wish of propagating the population of this universe."

The four brothers looked at each other and then turned simultaneously to their father; Brahma.

Sanaka; the eldest brother spoke thus, "My dear father, it is already known to us that you yourself was born from Lord Vishnu, so we wanted to live our lives devoted to Sri Vishnu because He is the Supreme Personality of the Godhead. Therefore we are unable to fulfil your wish of propagating the population."

Upon speaking thus, the Kumaras immediately vanished from the sight with explosion. Brahma flew into rage but he controlled his anger with great intelligence.

Bhaktivendata Swami stated that Lord Brahma has the capability of controlling his anger with his intelligence. If we humans wanted to control our anger, we need to do so using our mind and intelligence. A learned man is able to control the anger more efficiently compared to an uneducated man. This is a general rule. Education in this case means not going to school and learning the sciences, but is actually learning the philosophy of spirituality. This is the core of controlling anger. If anyone were able to control the anger, he is eligible to control his senses and if that is possible, he can be steady in the determination.

Controlling His emotion, Lord Brahma created ten beings from His mind, exactly like how he created the Kumaras, but the beings sprang as adults and not like mere babies as the Kumaras. These ten beings were known as 'Manas-Putras'. The word 'Manas-Putras' means mind sons. They were the original fathers of mankind but because they were created by Brahma, Hindus' refer Brahma as *Pitamaha*. It means grandfather. But as Brahma himself was created by Lord Vishnu, He is known as *PraPitamaha*. It means great grandfather. The Manas- Putras name were as follows; Narada, Pulastya, Marichi, Angiras, Pracetas, Pulaha, Kratuj, Vashista, Bhrigu and Atri.

"My dear sons, I created all of you to populate this entire universe, with your off springs, please do not say you cannot as the Kumaras that I created were unable to fulfil my wish." said Lord Brahma.

Marichi representing his siblings said, "My dear father, we will carry out your wish".

"Please bless us", said Vashista and all of them bowed except Narada. He said, "Father, I wish to dedicate my life to Lord Vishnu without getting married."

Lord Brahma after hearing this flew into rage. His eyes turned reddish but suddenly a powerful voice was heard across the newly formed universe.

"Listen here Brahma, Narada has My word that in this life he will live his entire life dedicated to Me", Lord Brahma understood that the voice belongs to Lord Vishnu.

"So be it Narada," replied Brahma slowly. Narada bowed his head to his father and travelled to the direction of Vaikuntha to see Lord Vishnu. However the other Manas- Putras vanished to carry out the order of propagating the universe. After instructing his sons, Lord Brahma returned to his lotus flower which is actually his planetary abode known as Brahmaloka.

It is told that various gods and goddess of numbering 33 million, and 840 000 creatures within this universe were all originated from the 'Manas-Putras'.

After the propagation of mankind and various beings, Lord Vishnu expanded Himself once more into much smaller Vishnu known as Ksirodakasayi Vishnu. The Ksirodakasayi Vishnu entered into each and every heart of the beings, including the lowborn animals like ant up to gods like Lord Brahma and Lord Shiva. Ksirodakasayi Vishnu is also known as the Paramatma; Supersoul. Thus, Lord Vishnu exists in our heart as Supersoul. He not only entered within the hearts of the beings but also within each and every atom that make up this universe. This fact is confirmed in the *Brahma-Samhita* that Lord Vishnu had entered within the atom.

The *Bhagavad- Gita* states; I am the source of all spiritual and material worlds. Everything emanates from Me.

No beings can fully understand Lord Vishnu's expansion, its purpose and the numbers. It is beyond anything, beyond the knowledge. Lord Krishna (8th incarnation of Lord Vishnu) says that it is possible that for a physicist to estimate the number of atoms that make up earth, but to estimate Lord Vishnu's various forms, activities and paraphernalia is totally impossible and out of question.

The creation of universes and various beings all originally came from Lord Vishnu. He is the utmost root cause of everything in this universe. Lord Vishnu is the supreme god that preserves this universe and He took numerous incarnations to preserve the universe from the hands of various demons.

NOTE:

In the eleventh chapter of *Bhagavad- Gita,* Lord Krishna explained the history of the universe briefly. Lord Brahma was born out of His navel. From Brahma, all living entities all over the universe are manifested.

The various Vedic literatures explained that there are innumerable universes and innumerable planets within each universe, and each planet is full of population of different varieties.

THE BIRTH TALE OF LORD GANESHA - GOD OF SUCCESS

In Hindu mythology, Ganesha is often known as the victory god. He is the son of the great Lord Shiva and Parvathi Devi. The tale of how the lord of success was born is narrated here.

Once upon a time in Kailash, Parvathi; the wife of Lord Shiva wanted to take a bath. Thus, she called upon a ghana who was plucking some flowers nearby. The ghana stopped his errand and walked towards Parvathi. Bowing his head, he said respectfully, "Devi, what are orders do you want me to carry out?"

Parvathi answered, "I wanted to take bath, so I want you to guard the entrance of this residential quarter and do not let anyone to enter until I finished bathing".

"Yes, devi, I will carry out your orders", said the ghana. Smiling, Parvathi entered her quarters to take bath. The ghana immediately murmured some magical words and in an eye blink, a stick appeared in his hands. He grinned as if the stick was a joke and walked up and down holding the iron stick once in a while whirling it.

After some time of guarding, the day came to an end and at this time the ghana saw Lord Shiva approaching to the private apartment seated on his favourite vehicle known as Nandi.

Nandi gracefully walked and stopped in front of the compound. Lord Shiva came down from the white bull, patted it as a sign of affection. At Shiva's touch, Nandi suddenly transformed into a young man. The young man bowed to the god and vanished. Lord Shiva while holding his trident, walked towards the entrance of his residential quarters when he was stopped by the ghana.

"Lord, your wife is bathing, and it is her order that no one can enter the quarters till she finished bathing", said the ghana in a trembling yet confident tone.

Shiva came near to the ghana. The ghana flinched as Shiva's body began to emanate power as the lord inched closer. Lord Shiva straightened his body and replied, "Have you forgotten who the master of Kailash is?" The ghana shook his head quickly as if it were to fall off.

"I can go wherever I like because this is my dominion" "Besides, Parvathi is my wife. Now, make way!".

The ghana had no choice but to let him enter. Thus, he stepped aside, bowing. Lord Shiva walked into his residence.

"Pheww, lucky Lord Shiva did not turn me into anything or curse me. It is my luck. Om Namo Shivaya!" said the ghana quietly and he walked to his residential quarters after a close encounter to the Lord's wrath. It is said that Lord Shiva can be pleased easily and at the same time he can get angry easily.

Shiva entered the apartment and saw Parvathi walking to her room holding her towel and her drenched sari. She is still wet from the bath and her breasts as well as her private parts were exposed. Upon seeing Shiva, Parvathi Devi grew ashamed because she is not properly dressed and her private parts are exposed. Although, Shiva is her husband, but Parvathi felt uncomfortable of her condition. She hung her head and quickly stormed into her room to change. While changing, she thought, "How can the ghana allow Lord Shiva to enter while I am bathing"

After a few days, Parvathi wanted to take bath again. "The earlier ghana that I asked him to guard the entrance failed in his job", Parvathi mumbled to herself. "I need to create my own ghana, whom will not deviate from the duty of guarding the entrance while I am bathing" thought Parvathi further.

Without wasting any time, Parvathi took a metal pot filled with sandalwood and made a statue of a boy from it. After completing the statue, she blew life to it. Some accounts stated that it was not Parvathi who gave life to the statue, but it was Lord Brahma himself.

Immediately the boy statue came alive and said, "Mother, you made me a body and gave me a life, tell me your wish and I will fulfil it no matter what happens".

Parvathi feeling overjoyed thus replied, "My son, I want to take bath so I want you to guard the entrance and do not allow anyone in until I finished bathing".

"If so is your wish, I will see it done, do not despair", replied the boy. "But mother, I want some food", said the boy rubbing his stomach. Parvathi smiled, "Ok, my son, your food is here", said Parvathi gently, carrying her palm. Light shone from her palm and a tray full of modhaka appeared.

The boy walked towards the tray and began to eat the modhaka. "Hmmm, it is delicious, what do you call it mother?"

"Modhaka" answered Parvathi as the boy began inhaling the Modhaka. "Ok, now I need to cleanse my body. Guard the entrance while you are eating", said Parvathi walking into her quarters before giving an axe to her son.

Parvathi vanished into her quarters to take bath and the boy started his duty of guarding the entrance. He armed himself with the axe and stood like a mountain.

For some time, the boy did not move away and continue guarding the entrance. Suddenly there was a lightning and thunder at the area. Lord Shiva appeared from nowhere clutching his celebrated trident known as *Trishula*.

Lord Shiva walked towards Parvathi's quarters and he saw a boy guarding the entrance. "Who is this boy, I have not seen him before in Kailash?" thought Shiva silently. Thinking that he is a ghana, Shiva walked passed the boy. The boy held up his hand and said strictly, "My mother is bathing. I cannot let anyone to enter."

"Boy, you have no idea what you are talking about. Parvathi is my wife. Now let me in", replied Shiva.

"No!" "My mother told me that not to let anyone to enter until she finished bathing." insisted the boy

"Boy, if Parvathi is your mother, I am your father. So, let me enter." said the lord.

The boy stubbornly said, "No!" "Be it anyone, I cannot deviate from my duty of guarding this entrance" "Now, go away!"

Lord Shiva flew into rage. His eyes turned red like hot copper and his third eye opened. Lord Shiva has three eyes. The third eye is located in the middle of his forehead. In Tamil language, it is known as *Netri-Kaan*. It is always closed but a great rage will cause it to open.

"Fool! You have no idea of whom you are against! For this I will teach a lesson that you will never forget!" shouted Lord Shiva angrily. The god clutched his trident tighter. It began to boil with energy that began to emanate from the pointed tips.

The boy snorted as if the trident was least of his worries and took arm with his axe prepared to defend himself. The boy held the axe powerfully and neatly. He gets in a battle mode; crouching his body low like a tiger as if he wanted to pounce on the lord.

Thus began a battle between the boy and Lord Shiva. The battle cause a severe earthquakes and howling wind in the universe. When this battle is going on, King Indra and the other gods were at that time at Brahmaloka. They were taking advices from the creator regarding the administration of this universe. The battle in Kailash causes the planet to sway like a ragged doll. The gods who were at their respective seats fall due to this severe shaking.

"What is going on?" demanded Indra angrily, picking up his crown which fell from his head just now. He stood and inspected Lord Brahma. Brahma closed his eyes for a moment.

"There is a battle raging in Kailash"

"Lord Shiva is combating with a boy", said Brahma pausing for a moment.

"A boy? Well this is surprising!" said Agnideva astonished.

"I think we should go to Kailash and see what is going on", suggested Indra quickly.

"No! The fight is in Lord Shiva's favour. No beings can win over Mahadeva. There is no need to worry and go to Kailash to see the fight. It will be just a waste of time", replied Brahma coolly. Indra nodded in respect.

"Please go to your respective duties", said Brahma. After Brahma gave order to the gods, immediately they vanished in blinding light from Brahmaloka.

At this time, Parvathi finished bathing and heard some noises. She called a lady servant and asked, "What is the loud noise? What is going on?"

A servant girl who was standing nearby answered, "My lady, your son is fighting with your husband to guard the entrance" "That is the cause of this noise."

Parvathi's heart bloomed with anger and said loudly, "What kind of act is this, my husband is against a boy?" "I must go and see his condition." Without properly dressing herself, the goddess stormed out of her quarter heading to the entrance.

The great battle was still going on. Lord Shiva was greatly surprised by the boy's strength. Actually, the strength of the boy is not surprising because he was made by Parvathi Devi.

Parvathi herself is an incarnation of Aadhi Sakthi. The great devotee by the name of Aabhirami Pattar said that it was Aadhi Sakthi who is responsible to provide strength to all the living beings. Sakthi means strength. So, the boy obtained the full strength and grace out of Aadhi Sakthi who is actually his mother; Parvathi.

However, in the end Shiva throws his trident with full strength. The boy blocked it with his axe, but his axe was chopped into half and the trident severed the boy's head from his body. The head and the body fall to the ground and the trident flew back to Shiva like a boomerang which the god captured it by extending his right hand. The battle was over. Satisfied at his victory, Shiva vanished from the sight and appeared at the summit of Kailash. Breathing deeply, he sat in meditation to control his anger.

Parvathi heard her son's cries, just when she wanted to go out to the scene of battle. Upon hearing the cries, she quickens her pace and arrived at the battleground to see her son's condition.

Unfortunately, what she saw was the head of her son severed from the body and blood everywhere. She couldn't see Lord Shiva anywhere.

"My son, I asked you to guard the entrance but you have left me!" lamented Parvathi sobbing. She crashed on the ground.

Choking on her tears, she breathed with utmost grief. Caressing her incapacitated child, Parvathi yelled, "Durga Devi, Kali Devi, come here at once!"

These goddesses namely Durga and Kali are the expansion of Parvathi. In other words, Parvathi called upon her own expansion.

An expansion of gods is quite similar with the concept of reflection but the expansion has the capability of acting by itself. In other words, an expansion has its own mind. Thus, it can be concluded that the expansion of a god is the incarnation or avatar.

Suddenly the clouds hovering Kailash darkened just like rainy season. The clouds suddenly combined and began to churn with lightening flashed across the horizon. All of a sudden there was some blinding light and out from the light came the two goddesses.

The goddess Durga Devi appeared clothed with her beautiful red sari and she is garlanded with flowers. Durga has eight hands and each of them is holding a bow, an arrow, a trident, a shield, a conch shell, a mace, glittering sword and a razor sharp disc. She breathed heavily with anger and her chest was moving up and down.

Beside her is the gigantic form of Kali Devi. She has four arms. Her eyes were bloodshot red and her tongue protrudes out. The goddess wore a garland made up of human skulls and a skirt made up of human hands. Her skin was dark blue. She held a curved sword known as *Khadga* in her left hand, a demon's head in her right upper hand and a bowl in her right lower hand. Blood was dripping from the head into the bowl and some dripped out of the bowl and spilled on the ground. The stains of blood which dripped on the ground were like acid. It created a hole in the ground which smoked. An aura of energy shone from these two goddesses body. They looked upon Parvathi with their terrible eyes.

Kali spoke in her powerful voice, "Why you have summoned us here, Parvathi?"

"I am grieving as my son is dead, killed by Lord Shiva himself. I want both of you to descend to earth and wreak chaos" instructed Parvathi still sobbing.

When Parvathi instructed them, they descended to earth and began to kill all the inhabitants. Indra at once sensed that earth is in big trouble. He called upon other gods. The other gods as they sensed their presences are required began to vanish from their respective planets.

"Why have you summoned us?" asked Yama representing other gods.

"Earth is in danger, we must go and save it, for it is our duty." said Indra, gulping some Soma juice and armed himself with his thunderbolt. Similarly other gods also armed with their respective weapons.

The gods descended on their chariots to earth. Indra saw that earth was laid bare and countless humans were lying here and there. Then he saw Durga hurling her trident to a group of screaming humans. The trident severed their heads. Their bodies fell like banana trees cut by the whirlwind. Kali was wreaking chaos not far away and shouts can be heard.

"How are we going to fight against Durga and Kali?" asked Vayu trembling. Indra led out huge sigh and said, "These gods are embodiment of Devi's power and anger. Only she can control them, no one can fight with them",

"Then let's go to her and ask her to do so," said Yama, holding his noose with his trembling hands.

"Ok, let's go to Kailash," concluded Indra after seeing Kali who appeared and started to drink all the blood of the fallen humans and began to dance on their mangled bodies. The gods vanished and appeared in Kailash which was brewing with storm.

The group of gods came to Parvathi who was still sitting and hugging her headless son. Indra bowed and said, "Parvathi, you are the mother to all the beings. Therefore please withdraw your incarnations from earth and bring balance to earth,"

"Indra, I will only withdraw my forces if and only if my son is revived," answered Parvathi crying. Indra turned from her looking very worried and faced other gods.

"The boy was killed by Lord Shiva's trident. No one can reattach the head." mumbled Indra rubbing his hands nervously. "If so, only Lord Shiva can revive the boy," answered Agni.

"Let us go and see Lord Shiva," suggested Varuna. Thus, all the gods went to his place of meditation which is the summit of Kailash.

"Lord Shiva, please deliver us from these calamities caused by Durga and Kali," prayed Indra and the other gods bowing and with folded hands.

Lord Shiva opened his eyes. "What is the problem? Why all of you are here?" he asked.

Indra narrated what was happening on earth. He furthur explained that Parvathi's grief was the source of this problem.

"Don't despair, I will look into it", replied Shiva, standing up. Gripping his trident, he vanished from the sight and appeared in front of Parvathi. The gods followed Shiva to see his furthur actions. Shiva saw that his wife was sitting beside the body of the boy which he beheaded; crying and her tears are like torrents of rain.

Shiva's heart suddenly filled with remorse for killing the boy. He blinked his lotus eyes and asked in a gentle voice, "Parvathi, why are you grieving?"

Parvathi looked at her husband's worried face. She hugged the dead boy tighter and answered in sad yet authorative voice, "Lord, you have mercilessly killed our son, so please revive him. If you do not abide, my two incarnations namely Durga and Kali will destroy the universe."

Hearing his wife's reply, Shiva led out a big sigh and said, "The head was severed by my trident. Don't you know that any being severed by my trident, there is no chance of reviving them?"

Parvathi answered, "I do not care, you must revive my son or else I will not be pacified."

Lord Shiva turned his head. "Come here," called Shiva to a frightened looking ghana. The ghana hurried and bowed. Lord Shiva without looking at him spoke, "Go to earth and bring forth the head of any organism that you first encountered. The head must lie facing the north direction. Bring another two or three ghanas to assist you".

The ghana called upon his friends and without wasting a moment, they vanished and appeared at earth.

"I suggest we go in the four directions. After two hours, we will meet here again." said a pencil slim ghana.

"I don't think so it is a good idea. Remember Kali and Durga are out there. It is better we stay together." replied a bearded ghana.

"Ok, whatever, we must not waste any more time", said another. The ghanas walked into a lush green forest. They walked for ages but could not find any beings.

"Look, there it's a dead elephant." shouted the slim ghana with excitement, pointing his index finger to the dead beast. "The head is facing north, I guess." Another ghana looked carefully at the head of the elephant and gazed up at the sky to locate the sun. "It sure is, now quick; we need to bring this head. There is no time to lose", shouted the thin ghana, walking towards the elephant followed by his companions.

"Om Namo Shivaya!" murmured the slim ghana. Suddenly an axe appeared from nowhere, floating in the air. The blade gleamed with sunlight.

He took the axe and with a powerful swing, severed the head from the body of the elephant. "Our job is done, let's go to Lord Shiva", the ghana said, holding the elephant's head with dripping blood. Without wasting a moment, the ghanas vanished and appeared in front of Lord Shiva who was still standing there like a statue. "My Lord, this is the head that we found", said the ghana bowed and handing the head to the lord.

Shiva extends his right hand, and out came some blinding light. The light engulfed the head and brought it to the headless boy who was laid on the ground by Parvathi. Using his mystic power, Lord Shiva connects the elephant head to the body. Once connected the elephant headed boy suddenly rises. He glanced around him and saw a large assembly of gods.

Parvathi was overjoyed and she threw her arms around the boy, who seemed surprised at his mother's behaviour. "Why are you crying mother?" he asked

"My dear son, after you have been killed by your father, you have been revived", answered Parvathi. He turned his head towards Lord Shiva who is still standing. The boy walked towards the Lord and sank on a knee,

"Father, without knowing you, I have mistakenly fought with you. Please forgive me.", said the elephant headed boy humbly.

Lord Shiva smiled and using his arms, he raised his son from the ground. Lord Shiva then replied, "My son, I forgive you. It is my fault that I acted harshly just now, but now, since you are my son, you shall be the leader of the ghanas. Thus, your name is Ganesha."

Lord Shiva continued, "You will be the first god to be worshipped in any religious ceremonies. You are the god of success and the remover of obstacles" Lord Shiva blessed him.

Lord Shiva held Ganesha's shoulder and brought him to Parvathi. Parvathi hugged her son. Feeling very happy, Parvathi decided to withdraw her forces. "Durga Devi, Kali Devi, please return," she called loudly. Suddenly Durga Devi with her trident and Kali appeared. Immediately all the gods including Lord Shiva bowed to these goddesses. Durga and Kali blessed Ganesha and disappeared. All the denizens from the other planets began to shower Lord Ganesha with different flowers, to celebrate his revival.

NOTE:

The eternal associates of Lord Shiva known as the ghanas are actually various ghosts and hobgoblins. Lord Shiva is therefore known as *Butha-nantha* (king of ghosts and denizens of inferno)

THE BIRTH TALE OF LORD KARTIKEYA - COMMANDER OF THE GODS

Lord Kartikeya is also known as Lord Muruga commonly. He is the second son of Lord Shiva and Parvathi and the younger brother of Lord Ganesha. Lord Skanda is widely regarded as Tamil god and is mostly worshipped in South India. The story of Lord Muruga came to existence mainly because of the appearance of the demon by the name of Surapadman.

Surapadman, when reached adult age thought, "The time is ripe enough for me to do severe penance to appease Lord Brahma". Generally, demons stick to worshipping Lord Brahma or Lord Shiva. It is very rare to find a demon praying to Lord Vishnu. After making up his mind, the demon made his way to a dense forest which was located near to his demoniac palace.

The forest was thick and in the middle of the forest is a tall mountain. Surapadman gazed at the mountain summit and whispered to himself, "It is a good spot to meditate. I will meditate there".

The forest is covered with many types of vegetation and various wild animals. However Surapadman was not afraid of these creatures and as he came across them, the animals ran helter skelter looking for protection.

Holding a sharp sword, Surapadman slashed the plants obstructing his way and continued to walk deeper into the forest.

Ultimately he reached the base of the mountain and gazed up. The mountain rose very high and its peak were covered with the clouds of King Indra. Smiling, the demon started to climb the mountain.

In an eye blink, he reached the top and saw lightning flashed every now and then. Without wasting any moment, Surapadman started to meditate concentrating his mind upon Lord Brahma. Rain began to fall but the demon neither flinched nor opened his eyes. Undisturbed by the severe rainfall, he continued his meditation.

For a very long time, Surapadman continued his meditation to the creator god although harassed by howling wind and torrents of rain, which were like piercing arrows.

The clouds were actually the representative of King Indra. Indra is the director of different clouds. The purpose of the king of heaven is to disrupt Surapadman's meditation. The reason is simple. As gods always wage wars against demons, so if any demon were to get some boon, the gods will be in a dangerous situation. Thus to prevent this situation from happening, Indra tries to disturb the demon's meditation by sending trials and tribulations.

Lord Brahma could not tolerate any longer the calling of Tarakasuran. The creator opened his eyes and simultaneously sighed, after a moment he disappeared from his abode. He appeared in front of the demon, levitating among the dark clouds, held up his right hand which was decorated by the symbol of sacred Om. Brahma said in a gentle voice, "Surapadman I am here, open your eyes".

Being ordered by Lord Brahma, Surapadman opened his eyes slowly and looked. He saw Brahma with radiating effulgence and looking very brilliant. Surapadman immediately stood and bowed his head, folding his hands. He said in a coarse voice, "Lord Brahma, you are the greatest among the *Trimurtis*, please grant me a boon."

Brahma smiled and replied "Ask whatever boon you desire within my power".

"My dear Lord Brahma, please grant me the boon of immortality". Hearing this, Brahma widened his pupils, and replied in a gentle but powerful voice, "Surapadman, don't ask the boon that I cannot grant you, every beings will die eventually, no beings can escape from death".

The words of Brahma are of a fact. No beings can escape from death, not even the gods. When this particular cosmic manifestation comes to an end, every beings including Brahma will die. Only Vishnu will continue to exist even with the annihilation of this universe. Lord Vishnu exists before this creation of the universe, He exists during the creation and even after the ultimate destruction of this material universe, and He will continue to exist. In other words, the true immortal is Lord Vishnu. The other gods simply have very long duration of life, and will meet their end when the time comes.

Surapadman frowned, he rubbed his chin and replied "Lord Brahma, if so that is the case, then please grant me the boon, that I can only be killed by Lord Shiva's son."

Surapadman thought that since Lord Shiva wife had passed away, and Shiva is an ascetic, so the question of him marrying again were totally out. Thus there is no chance that there will be a son born from Shiva.

"Then so be it," answered Lord Brahma and he vanished in a blinding flash of light accompanied with a clap of thunder.

Taraka beamed and without wasting any time, he climbed down the hill in a flash. He made his way to his demonic city and at once started his action of conquering the universe.

Surapadman conquered each and every planet. He drove King Indra out of the heavenly kingdom and harassed the beings on this earth.

During Surapadman rampage, Lord Shiva was meditating deeply due to his wife; Shakthi's death. However Shakthi was reborn as Parvathi to the daughter of the Himalayan Mountains. Parvathi as she grew up was told by various gods and sages that she is the incarnate of Aadhi Shakthi and so is destined to be the wife of Lord Shiva once more.

Aadhi Shakthi is the primeval energy that is actually the chief of internal potency of Lord Vishnu. In other words, Parvathi is actually the younger sister of Vishnu. Parvathi, answering to fate, that she must unite with Lord Shiva when she reached marriageable age, and she is very aware of her great destiny. Thus Parvathi ventured into a dense forest whereby is rumoured to be the place where Lord Shiva meditates.

Upon reaching the spot, Parvathi saw Shiva seated on a great big rock, wearing a tiger skin and the god's skin was bluish. His face was in deep concentration and on his forehead was applied ash in three lines, which Hindus' call as *vibuthi*. His eyes were closed and he is very deeply into the world of meditation, as Parvathi observed Lord Shiva's powerful weapon; the trident was literally standing at his side. His chest moves up and down as his lungs was filled with forest air and defiled rhythmically.

Parvathi blinked. She was clearly hesitant to approach the god of destruction. However, she steadied herself and walked slowly towards the lord. Standing in front of him, trembling, and with folded hands she said, "Lord Shiva, please open your eyes and see me as I am now at your service". Shiva opened his lotus like eyes and he saw Parvathi kneeling with both her knees in front of him.

He asked, "My dear lady, who are you?"

"I am the daughter of the Himalayan Mountains named Parvathi. My aim is to serve you"

Shiva seemed to be surprised, and replied in a soft voice, "How are you going to do that Parvathi?" Hearing the god's question, Parvathi answered, "My dear lord, let me collect the flowers and decorate this place, Let me pour water on you to have you cleansed. Let me be your slave until you finished your meditation"

"If that is your purpose, please be free to carry it out", replied Shiva and immediately closed his eyes, entering the world of meditation. After being permitted by Lord Shiva, Parvathi began her service. Every morning she collected various forest flowers and decorated the spot. Parvathi also collected water from a nearby running stream and bathed the god, thus cleaning him. Besides this she also did many other numerous services.

Time passed on and Parvathi still continued her service for Shiva. Her actions were noticed by other gods watching from the clouds. They went observing her for many years and at the same time the demon Surapadman continued ravaging the universe in his great terror campaign.

After many years, King Indra and other gods had grew weary in observing the same mundane scene; Lord Shiva meditating and

Parvathi continued to do services for Him. The condition of the universe is very critical. The demon grew powerful as the day goes by. Unable to tolerate any longer, King Indra stood authoritatively over the gods. He wield his weapon of choice; the thunderbolt and threw a sweeping gaze to his brethren. The lord of thunderclouds addressed them, "We have waited for a long time for the union of Lord Shiva and Parvathi but it doesn't seem that they will fall for each other" Indra said in a very loud and disappointing tone.

"So, what can we do?" asked Varunadeva quickly. Other gods kept silent. Seeing them keeping quiet, "We must make them fall in love so that they will marry and eventually have a son that will vanquish the demon" the lord of water answered to his own question in a hushed tone.

Upon hearing Varuna's words, Kamadeva; the god capable of inducing lusty desire and sexual arousal stood, holding his bow which was made of sugarcane, he spoke in a confident tone, "I can make Lord Shiva fall for Parvathi easily". King Indra and the gods fixed their gaze on Manmadha who looked extremely confident with his ability.

"If so, you should travel to Lord Shiva's place and carry out the act immediately," replied Indra as he stood holding his weapon, *vajrayudha* and disappeared from the sight. Upon seeing King Indra disappear, other gods also disappeared. Kama; armed with his sugarcane bow and appeared at Shiva's site of the meditation in the forest.

The cupid saw that Lord Shiva was lost in meditation and Parvathi serving him with by throwing flowers on him. Smiling, Kamadeva quietly hid behind a large tree. Then, he withdrew his bow which is made of sugarcane and fixed his arrow of love. Kamadeva took a deep breath and aimed at the heart of Lord Shiva.

Fate took turn to play as Kamadeva let the arrow go; Lord Shiva suddenly opened his eyes, including his fearsome third eye. Out of the third eye, fire sprayed fiercely just like out from a sprayer burning down the arrow and Kamadeva. Out of pain, Kamadeva screamed and eventually the god of love was reduced into ashes within seconds. Parvathi upon seeing the ghastly scene fell upon Shiva and begged him to stop his fiery attack.

All of a sudden, the third eye closed and Shiva, ignoring the death of Kama, returned to his meditation as if nothing happened. King Indra and other gods were observing from sky groaned when their plan to unite Lord Shiva and Parvathi failed.

"What are we going to do now?" asked Vayu still looking down from the heaven seeing Kama's demise. "I don't know, we need to wait", murmured Indra. Indra of all gods should have known that Lord Shiva is the master of this material nature and its modes. He certainly cannot be subjugated by a lesser god. Indra felt bad for sending Kamadeva to his death. He should have known that the act of Lord Shiva falling in love is something impossible. And now god of love is dead.

The fiery sparks which are lava that have emanated from Lord Shiva's third eye continued to travel, as if have life of its own. The lava flow from the place, downwards like mercury liquid, destroying trees and other animals fled in fear.

King Indra realised the danger of lava that emanated from Lord Shiva's third eye. The king of heaven said to the fire god. "Agni, go at once and contain the lava's heat with your power."

Agnideva closed his eyes and concentrated deeply to reduce the lava's destructive temperature. Then, he opened his eyes and replied miserably, "Indra, I can't do it."

The king of heaven looked mystified. "Why do you say so?" he asked. "I don't know, the heat is too great, no one could diminish the power," answered Agni. "Then, what did you do?" asked Indra worried.

"I hand it over to the River Ganges," answered Agni.

River Ganges carried the fiery lava with her streams. "I can't carry the heat any longer." she said panting after some time. Ultimately she deposited the lava in a forest of reeds called as Sara Vana Bhava. The lava cooled down and solidified into six handsome babies. The babies floated on six lotus flowers which magically appeared.

There happened when the Kirtika sisters, numbering six came to the forest to collect reeds. One of the sisters saw there were babies in lotuses, floating. She exclaimed, "My dear sisters, look there!"

The sisters gazed at the direction and saw those babies. One of them said, "Who are these babies? They are looking so cute".

The other siblings kept quiet until the eldest of the sisters voiced, "I think it is better that each of us take these babies than to leave them here," she said as she bent and picked one of the babies in her arms. Her siblings copied her actions.

The Kirtika sisters took the babies home. There was no one in their hut as the sisters' husband went to forest to practice severe austery. "We must take care of these babies", said one of the sisters putting the baby on the floor.

"I guess you are right." said another sister. "There is no chance of leaving these beautiful babies in the forest. Our husband is not here; maybe these babies will grow by the time. Until that we must take care of them. What all of you say?" Her siblings nod their head in great anticipation. And the Kirtika sisters took care of each baby for quite some time.

One fateful day, the sisters' husband who went to forest to practice meditation came home after finishing his businesses. He had no idea that the Kirtika sisters and their founding of the babies.

Once he reached home, he opened the door and said, "My dear Kirtika sisters, I have returned." gazing around the hut. His gaze stopped when he saw six babies playing on the floor. Breathing heavily, he shouted, "Kirtika sisters! Come here at once and explain this incident!" Upon hearing the angry voice of their husband, the sisters looked at each other alarmingly, sensing trouble. Without wasting any time, the sisters rushed to their husband who was standing in the middle of the house, fuming and staring at those babies.

"What is the matter?" asked the sisters in unison. "Who are these babies?" questioned their husband pointing at the babies with his finger as one of the babies begins to advance towards him.

"We found them at the Sara Vana Bhava forest," answered the eldest sister.

"No, I think you are lying to me!" thundered the man. "All of you have committed adultery when I was away and as a result, these babies were born to each of you," he continued. He moved backwards to the door.

"No, that is not true!" one of the Kirtika sisters replied but the man held up his hand, signalling her to stop.

"I have no idea what all of you did when I was absent." he yelled angrily standing at the door. Pausing a moment, he withdrew a deep breath and exclaimed loudly "For this offence, I curse all of you to turn into stars!" Suddenly, he thundered out of his house.

The sisters lamented. "Why is this thing happen to us?" mumbled one of them sobbing. Others stood still like a sad statues.

All of a sudden, the hut swayed like being blown by strong wind. The Kirtika sisters hugged each other in exparastion. Their flowers on their heads began to fall. "What is going on?!" screamed the eldest sister.

The hut shone with blinding light and out of it, Lord Shiva and his newlywed consort, Parvathi appeared in front of the sisters. The sisters bowed.

Lord Shiva smiled and said gently, "My dear Kirtika sisters, these babies were my sons as they were born out of my third eye," he gestured to the six babies who began to crawl towards Parvathi now. Parvathi sat and she hugged the babies.

"I knew that your husband had cursed all of you. The curse of your husband cannot be withdrawn but I assure you that your service will be continued to be remembered by people when they worship my son. Thus his name will be Kartikeya." explained Shiva

The Kirtika sisters kept silent for a second. One of them said happily, "Lord, we are honoured to take care of your sons. Permit us to receive our punishment", she continued. The sisters touched Shiva and Parvathi's feet and circumambulated the lord. After this, they were suddenly drawn into the sky.

After the deliverance of Kirtika sisters, Parvathi was thinking of how she could carry all six sons with her.

Understanding his consort's troubled mind, Shiva told her, "My dear, why don't you combine all these babies into a single body and of six heads." Nodding at her husband's suggestion, Parvathi used her mystic power and combined those babies into a single body and six heads.

Taking her six headed baby in her arms, Parvathi said, "Since you have six faces, you will be named as Aarumugham. 'Aaru' means six and 'mugham' means face. Since he is very beautiful, he is also known as Muruga.

Shiva and Parvathi vanished from the hut in a flash of light, taking their son to Mount Kailash to further nurture and prepare him for battle against Surapadman.

The Kirtika sisters, who became the stars, form the constellation Pleiades in the night sky. So, when you look upon Pleiades remember the Kirtika sisters' service.

NOTE:

The constellation Pleiades is a group of six stars, but the modern scientist stated that it was made up of seven stars.

The Story Of Jaya And Vijaya - The Twin Guardians Of Vaikuntha

Once upon a time, the four Kumaras - namely Sanaka, Sananta, Sanandana and Sanat-Kumara wanted to see Lord Vishnu and clarify some things about Absolute Truth.

Everyone is searching for truth. If there is any truth in this material world, the truth itself comes from the Absolute Truth, Lord Vishnu Himself. Absolute Truth is the origin of everything and it created the mind, senses and intelligence. A specific Vedic literature known as the *Upanisads* described about Absolute Truth. It is said that the Absolute Truth is above material qualities. It is known as *nirguna*.

They started their journey by moving out from their planetary abode; known as Janaloka. Janaloka is a planet where sages and ascetics live. It is situated above the Svargaloka planets (upper planetary system).

Due to their excellent capacity, they travelled in outer space and in no time they reached the atmosphere of Vaikuntha. It is explained by Bhaktivedanta Swami that the Kumaras and great ascetics like Narada hardly ever travel on land as they perpetually travel in space visiting different planets in order to educate the beings that their business in the world is to reinstate them in the position of devotional service to Lord Vishnu.

Upon reaching the Vaikuntha's atmosphere, they descended smoothly and set their foot on the land. When the Kumaras landed, the planet Vaikuntha itself trembled slightly as if it was having an earthquake. The brothers made a beeline to the entrance gate.

The planet Vaikuntha has seven entrances before the private quarters of Lord Vishnu which is the ocean of milk where He lies on His snake-bed known as Ananta-Sesa.

The Kumaras walked through the entrances at ease. As they approached to each entrance gate, the golden gates opened automatically outwards as if welcoming them in.

Eventually, the four brothers passed through the six gates and reached the seventh gate; which is the last entrance. Unlike the previous gates, the seventh gate was guarded by two men in whom they were armed with a sharp, curved sword and a golden shield. Those men were also appeared to be as strong as a thunderbolt and their eyes were very fearful.

The Kumaras walked through the seventh gate ignoring the gaze of the two guards. However when they came near to the gate, the two men blocked the entrance with their swords.

Spontaneously, the four brothers stepped back in surprise simultaneously. Then, the brothers headed by Sanaka (eldest brother) asked, "Who are you people and why are you blocking the entrance".

"I am Jaya and he is my brother by the name of Vijaya. We are both the guardians of the planet Vaikuntha, particularly to the private quarters of Lord Vishnu," told one of the men in a strong voice, brandishing his sharp sword.

Sanaka said gently, "Jaya and Vijaya; the twin guardians of Vaikuntha, we are the four Kumaras." "I am Sanaka. These are my brothers Sananta, Sanandana and Sanat-Kumara.", pointing to each of his siblings with his small babyish index finger. "We have come here to seek an audience with Sri Hari. Kindly allow us to enter." Sanaka continued in a very gentle voice.

Jaya and Vijaya exchanged looks. Vijaya laughed loudly causing Sanaka to look confused. The guardian of Vaikuntha put forward his fierce face to Sanaka and replied in a sarcastic tone, "Sri Hari is now resting and He will not see anybody."

"Lord Vishnu will make time for His devotees. Besides there is no certain time constrains that when we can see Him or not." Sanandana replied in an angry tone.

"That is correct, brother", Sanantana said.

"Now, make way for us and do not waste our time", said Sanaka in a slightly annoyed tone.

Upon hearing Sanaka's strong words, Jaya immediately pointed the tip of his sword to Sanaka's chin. Sanaka did not flinch and he stood like a statue; not moving even an inch. Jaya said, "Now listen here, you kids, when I said that Lord Vishnu is not making any time to see you that means He is certainly not making any time for you. So let me suggest a way, all four of you can go back or else I shall smith your heads with my sword. Now make your choice."

The words of Jaya that referred the Kumaras as kids are actually a fact. Due to the great power of the Kumaras' they appear as mere babies although they were the oldest beings existent being born directly from Lord Brahma when the time dawns. The guardians of Vaikuntha thought that they can scare the Kumaras by using harsh words and by threathening them. In other words, Jaya and Vijaya mistook the Kumaras to be unimportant personalities to seek an audience with the Supreme Personality of Godhead.

Bhaktivendata Swami said that the four Kumaras are so gentle and they do not distinguish between enemies and friends. They have an ideal character and are topmost devotees of Lord Vishnu, known as *Maha- Bhagavata* (first class devotee).

However gentle they are, the twin guardians of Vaikuntha planet is clearly testing their patience. Thus, upon hearing the threatening words of Jaya; the four Kumaras felt greatly agitated. Their eyes turned reddish as if fire was burning in their sockets.

The brothers said in unison in a strong rumbling voice; as grave as thundercloud, "Dear Jaya and Vijaya; twin guardians of Vaikuntha, both of you made mistake by not permitting us to enter and seek audience with Sri Hari! For this offence, both of you will take birth on earth."

The words of the Kumaras' were very powerful as Vaikuntha itself shook. Sri Vishnu, who was lying on His snake-bed, meditating in the *yoga-nindram* position, opened His eyes.

He understood that shaking of the planet were actually the effect of the Kumaras words. Lord Vishnu sensed that His best devotees were angry and so He vanished from His bed and appeared in front of the Kumaras with four celebrated symbols, namely the disc known as *Sudarshana Chakra*, the lotus flower, the mace known as *Kaumodaki* club and the conch shell which was known as *Pancajanya*.

Upon seeing Him, the twin guards as well as the four brothers immediately bowed. Lord Vishnu smiled at their actions and blessed them. He then asked, "Why is this commotion?"

Upon hearing Sri Vishnu's question, Jaya immediately narrated the incident of them refusing the entry of four Kumaras and as a result they were cursed by the quardlet brothers.

Vijaya pleaded, "Lord, by foolishness we have underestimated the capacity of Your bona fide devotees, taking them as mere children. However we have realised our mistake. Please my Lord, remove this curse"

Lord Vishnu is the Supersoul. He is within the hearts of the Kumaras as well as the twin guardians. However, he wanted to hear the incident from the twin guardians themselves.

After hearing the incident of cursing of the Kumaras', the Supreme Personality of Godhead replied in gentle voice, "Jaya and Vijaya, both of you must take note that the curses of the Kumaras cannot be lifted".

"However, I can offer you two choices to lessen the effect of the curse", continued Sri Hari.

"What are the offers, Lord?" asked Jaya and Vijaya simultaneously and enthusiastically.

Vishnu smiled and replied, "As the curses foretold, both of you must take birth on earth, but both of you may choose whether you wanted to take birth on earth for seven times as My devotees or both of you may choose to take birth three times on earth as My enemies"

Jaya spoke quickly, "Lord, we cannot stay away from You for seven births, so we might as well take three births as Your enemy"

"Very well, so both of you shall take three births as My enemy and will be killed by Me. After completing three births, both of you will be re-installed as My doorkeepers".

After hearing the Lord's words, Jaya and Vijaya disappeared from Vaikuntha to take birth on Earth. The four Kumaras praised Lord Vishnu for His wise decision. They then clarified their matters with the Lord. After finishing their business, the Kumaras excused themselves from Vaikuntha and returned to their abode. Lord Vishnu also went back to His meditation.

NOTE:

The three times Jaya and Vijaya took birth on Earth are as follows:

1st BIRTH: Jaya took birth as Hirayangkasha and Vijaya as Hirayangkashipu. Lord Vishnu took separate incarnation to kill them. In Varaha incarnation, Hirangkasha was killed and in Narasimha incarnation, Hiranyangkashipu was killed.

2nd BIRTH: Jaya was born as Ravana and Vijaya as Khumbakarna. Both were destroyed by Lord Rama.

3rd BIRTH: Jaya was incarnated as Shisupala and Vijaya as Dantavakra. Both were killed by Lord Krishna.

THE BREAKING OF PINAKA BOW BY LORD RAMA AND THE CURBING OF ARROGANCE OF LORD PARASHURAMA

Once upon a time, during Tretha Yuga, Lord Vishnu incarnated Himself as Ramachandra, the son of the King Dasaratha which originates from the sun planet.

When Ramachandra reached his teenage years, the sage Vishvamitra came to the court of King Dasaratha and brought Rama and his brother, Lakshmana to his hut. Both of the brothers followed Vishvamitra to his place of residence, various demons attacked them. Sri Rama and Lakshmana killed them all using their arrows.

Feeling grateful, Vishvamitra taught Rama and Lakshmana about the Vedic literatures and various arts such as art of fighting and composing music.

One day fine day, Vishvamitra said, "My dear Rama and Lakshmana, today I will take you to the kingdom of Janaka."

Rama asked, "O great sage, what is the purpose we are going there?"

"King Janaka is organizing a svayamvara ceremony for his daughter, Sitadevi. It is a good opportunity for you to marry her as you are aging," responded Vishvamitra.

"As you wish, sage," Rama said respectfully.

"Good, we will move now", said Vishvamitra happily.

Vishvamitra, Rama and Laksmana journeyed to kingdom Mithala where the ceremony was held.

Rama and Laksmana were the incarnations of Supreme Personality of Godhead, Vishnu. Thus, their hairs were dazzling like sun. As Vishvamitra, Rama and Laksmana arrived; the citizens of Mithila began to admire the brothers' beauty.

When they entered the palace, it was engulfed with glaring effulgence that is emanating from Rama and Lakshmana. King Janaka who was sitting on the throne, as soon he saw the trio had arrived, he immediately stood up along with his ministers and secretaries to receive Vishvamitra, Rama and Lakshmana. King Janaka bowed his head in front of Vishvamitra and offered his respectful obeisance.

"My dear sage, what can I do for you," he asked in a sweet voice.

Vishvamitra smiled and said, "King Janaka, I have brought the sons of King Dasaratha, namely Rama and Lakshmana so that they can participate in the svayamvara ceremony."

King Janaka tilted his head and looked at Rama. "Rama is certainly suitable to marry Sitadevi. His features were very beautiful exceeding cupid personality", he thought.

Janaka smiled and replied, "The ceremony is tomorrow, so please make yourself at home." Thus Vishvamitra, Rama and Laksmana stayed for a night in the palace, waiting for tomorrow svayamvara.

The day came for the ceremony. The trio entered the palace and sat at their respective seats. Rama saw many kings from all various kingdoms came to the ceremony.

Rama also saw a big black bow placed on a big table in the middle of the palace and he also caught a quick glimpse of Sita, who was standing beside her father holding a garland of flowers.

Sitadevi looked very beautiful. Her face emited some kind of ray whereas her eyes her eyes were like petals of flowers. Her white teeth sparkled like pearls and with raised breasts, thin hips, she looked very magnificent. Sita saw Rama among the princes and immediately attracted to him. She decided to marry only Rama.

Suddenly, King Janaka stood. All the chatters and bubbles of the princes suddenly came to a halt.

"I welcome all of you to Mithala," he said opening his arms widely.

"The svayamvara ceremony today will determine whether you are worthy enough to marry Sita, and for that you need to string this Pinaka bow," he continued, showing his hand to the enormous bow on the table.

"Sir, I have never heard of this Pinaka bow", whispered Lakshmana at once to Vishvamitra.

Vishvamitra whispered back, "The Pinaka bow is the personal weapon of Lord Shiva, given by him to Lord Parashurama. When Parashurama went to the Himalaya Mountains to meditate, he gave this bow to King Janaka for safekeeping until he return from his penance."

"What?! Lord Shiva's bow?!" asked Lakshmana astonished. "How is it possible for Rama to string it?" questioned Lakshmana to Vishvamitra.

"It is impossible for mere mortal to carry out his task," replied Vishvamitra confidently. "But, Rama is not a mortal, both of you are the incarnate of Sri Vishnu." "He is very capable, of course stringing the Pinaka bow is not a very big problem for Rama", continued Vishvamitra.

While they are talking, many kings tried to string the bow. However, none of them can even move it from the table. In the other words, how hard they tried one after another, to carry the bow, the bow remain steadfast and did not move even an inch. Thus, they returned to their seats feeling disappointed. Janaka smiled and addressed the crowd, "Anyone else wanted try?"

"Let me do it!" a voice louder than thunder suddenly boomed at the entrance. Everyone turned to look who it was. It seems that Ravana, had come to the ceremony. He was strong and his footsteps were heroic which shook the earth. All the kings kept quiet seeing the powerful demon lord.

Ravana walked to the bow and asked arrogantly, "This is the task?"

"Yes you must ...." said Janaka but Ravana gestured him to stop.

Ravana flexed his mighty muscled and grabbed the bow. With full strength, he carried the bow, or at least he tried because the bow only moved a few inches and when Ravana let it go, the bow fall back to the table with a loud thud.

Ravana felt extremely flabbergasted and without saying a word, he stormed out of the palace and abroad his *pushphaka vimana* which immediately flew into the open air.

"Now, it is your turn Rama," said Vishvamitra to Rama who was sitting beside. Rama rose from his seat, paid respect to Vishvamitra and bowed to King Janaka. Rama walked to the bow stealing the gaze of the princes.

He placed his strong hand on the bow and very easily carried it like a toy. Audience gasped but Vishvamitra, Lakshamana, Janaka and Sitadevi smiled. Rama held the bow with his foot and attempted to string the Pinaka bow. However, the bow suddenly broke with great tumultuous sound. The sound of the breaking of the bow travelled in four directions - namely north, south, east and west.

Without wasting anytime, Sitadevi descended from the stage and garlanded Rama among many kings. She knew that Rama is the original Vishnu and is fit to be her husband.

The audience showered flowers on them and shouted, "All glory to you, Rama!"

Thus after winning the hands of Sita, Rama married her according to Vedic ritualistic principles at Mithila kingdom. After marriage, they made way to Rama's kingdom known as Ayodya.

King Janaka arranged that thousands of maidservants to accompany the newly- wed couple. This is the way of marriage system opted by *ksatriyas* (kings and administrators). When a *ksatriya* is married, dozens of the bride's young girl friends will go to the king or price's kingdom. As Rama is the crowned prince of Ayodya, he brought home many girls along his wife.

The bride and bridegroom were passing along the roads, and were accompanied by different kind of musical instrument playing. Just as the procession was passing very pleasingly when a miraculous sound vibrated from the sky, "Who on earth can break the Pinaka Bow?!"

The people of the procession gasped as they frantically turned their head in attempt to locate the sound. Vishvamitra closed his eyes and opened within a second. "There is no use of standing here. Better we move on, before he comes", said the sage uncomfortably.

"Who?" asked Rama.

"Me!!" boomed a loud voice. Rama narrowed his eyes as he saw a shadow dropped from the sky. It is a man armed with an axe and he stood like a mountain.

"Who are you?!" asked Lakshmana as he walked forward gripping his bow. The man held up his palm, just like a traffic police. Lakshmana froze. Not only him but the entire procession froze including Vishvamitra as if the time stopped. However Rama is not affected by the man's mystic power.

"Who are you and what do you want?" asked Rama annoyingly.

"I am none other than the great Parashurama!" answered the man whirling his axe.

Rama's pupil dilated. He had heard the story of Parashurama who slaughtered all the *ksatriyas* around the world for twenty one times. Parashurama is actually the sixth incarnation of Lord Vishnu. He is certainly a terror to behold to *ksatriyas*.

"Sir, May I kindly ask why you have stopped us?" inquired Rama humbly.

"I am the strongest warrior on earth and no human can carry the Pinaka bow as far as I am concerned." began Parashurama. "I have no idea how you do it", he continued suspiciously. Rama kept very quiet.

Seeing the silence of Rama, the sage murmured some words. Suddenly, a bow appeared from the sky and rests on Parashurama's palm. He gripped the bow strongly and said in a commanding voice,

"If you are very capable, string this Vishnu bow. If you succeed, I will let you pass but if you fail, I will kill everyone who is present here."

Rama got very angry. He bowed to Parashurama and without any warning, he snatched the bow. In a second he joined the string to the both ends of the bow. Parashurama narrowed his eyes. However, Rama did not hand over the bow, but he took an arrow and aimed at the sage's heart.

Parashurama grew very uncomfortable. Suddenly, bright light came out from his body illuminating all directions. That effulgent light merged into the body of Lord Rama. The great warrior, Parashurama suddenly understood that the incarnation of Rama is definitely more powerful and since the purpose of his avatar is over, thus the bright light (essence of Vishnu) left his body merges with Rama's body.

Parashurama said humbly, "Without knowing that you are an incarnate of Vishnu, I had foolishly intercepted your journey. Please forgive me."

"Parashurama, I forgive you but as the purpose of your avatar is over, please don't interfere anymore with this mortal world," replied Rama gently.

Parashurama bowed to Rama and it a blink of an eye, he disappeared.

Lord Rama aimed the arrow to the sky with the Vishnu's bow and shot it. The arrow flew to the sky and never returned to the world. Ramayana tells us that the arrow will continue to fly all over the universe but will return to earth when the time ends.

NOTE:

The Pinaka bow belongs to Shiva. Since Lord Parashurama studied martial arts under Lord Shiva, this is one of the weapons given by Shiva to Parashurama.

Lord Parashurama is one of the celebrated immortals (*chiraanjeevi*) of Hinduism. He is still living in India on the Mahendra hills.

THE TALE OF LORD KRISHNA AND WEIGHING SCALE

When we look upon various Vedic literatures, Lord Vishnu descends on earth to destroy the miscreants and to protect the virtuous. The *Bhagavad-Gita* states that whenever there are discrepancies in the regulative principles of mans' religious life and when there is a prominent rise of irreligion, the Supreme Lord descends. When He descends from the eternal spiritual universe (Vaikhuntha planets) to this material world, we say that He incarnates and the forms are known as *avathars* or incarnations.

The Vishnu Purana lists twenty five incarnations of Lord Vishnu, but only ten incarnations is of utmost important. These ten were known as the *dashaavathar*. The *dashaavathar* according to numerical order is: Matsya (fish), Kurma (tortoise), Varaha (boar), Narasimha (man-lion), Vamana (dwarf brahmana), Parashurama (Rama with axe), Rama (Prince of Ayodya), Krishna (cowherd boy), Buddha (Enlightened One), Kalki (messiah).

This tale concerns with Lord Krishna. He is the most powerful of all Vishnu incarnations. Lord Vishnu descends as Krishna at the end of Dvapara Yuga 5000 years ago.

The Supreme Personality of Godhead remained on earth for approximately 125 years. During that period, He performs extraordinary feats to establish religious principles. One of such feat regarding two of His wives namely Rukmini and Sathyabhama is narrated here.

Krishna had 16108 wives. His first wife is none other than an incarnation of Lakshimiji herself. Goddess Lakshmi is the wife of Lord Vishnu. Whenever her husband descends, she will descend too. Similarly since Vishnu is Krishna so Lakshmi is Rukmini. Lord Krishna's second wife is Sathyabhama; goddess Bhumidevi's incarnation or the Earth's incarnation. However other than these two wives, Lord Krishna has another 16106 wives.

Lord Krishna has the capability to expand himself. The expansion of Lord Krishna is beyond human speculation. According to Bhaktivedanta Swami, through the knowledge of mystic power, one can learn to expand himself. However since Lord Krishna is the master of all mystic powers (Yogesvara), He can expand unlimitedly. Thus, He expanded into 16108 Krishnas in order to associate with each of His wife.

Therefore, He stays simultaneously with Rukmini in her palace quarters and with Sathyabama in her quarters. However neither Rukmini nor Sathyabama knew that Krishna is simultaneously associating with them. Rukmini thought that Krishna is 24 hours with her and Sathyabama thought similarly.

One day, as Rukmini was taking a stroll in the garden, she saw Krishna was sitting on a couch, eating and joking with Sathyabama. Rukmini flew into rage and said to herself, "Krsna had cheated me! Saying that He wanted to go out due to some political matter but

He is now enjoying with Sathyabama! Why should He lie to me?" she continued. Her eyes were wet with tears and her make-ups were washed. Feeling extremely frustrated, she ran to her quarters, crying.

Sathyabama on the other hand began to feel proud, thinking that herself to be most fortunate women in the Universe due to being to being favoured by the company of Krishna. She become as proud as she thought Krsna is a hen-pecked husband. Sathyabama said to herself, "Krsna now attached to me, not Rukmini. Rukmini has lost her ability and privileage to be with Krsna and she's not deserved to be with Him."

The thinking of Sathyabhama that Lord Krishna is attached to her is incorrect. Lord Krishna is never attached to anyone. Lord Krishna is the supreme renouncer. He always self satisfied (*atmarama*) and does not require anything to please himself. He derives pleasure by himself.

Since He is the Supersoul, Lord Krishna understood everything. Bhaktivedanta Swami explained that Sri Krishna does not like His devotee to be proud. If any of His devotees is proud, by some tactic He will remove the pride.

When a person becomes proud, his senses are blocked, so he cannot be steady in his determination. When this happens, he will fall from a stage of devotee to the stage of householder. In other words, he will get entangled in this material world once more.

"Sathyabhama had become proud! I will remove the pride now!" thought Lord Krishna. Thus, in order to exhibit His causeless mercy and to curb Sathya's false pride, he decided to enact a play. By Sri Krishna's will, the great sage Narada appear in front of Rukmini's quarters. Narada found her crying.

Narada said, "Mother, why are you weeping like a child?"

"My dear Narada, Krsna had lied to me in order to enjoy the company of Sathyabama!" "How dare He do this to me?" "Does He lose his interest in me?" Rukmini lamented in front of Narada.

Narada said, "My dear mother, please be assured that Sri Krishna will return to you. This is my assurance." After satisfying Rukmini with sweet words, the great sage Narada disappeared from the sight and appeared in front of Sathyabama who was sitting on the couch alone not realising Narada had come. Narada could not find Lord Krishna anywhere, and thought, "I will start my play now".

Narada let out some sort of deep growling from his throat. The sound startled Sathya, and she turned her head only to see the sage standing beside her. She stood up quickly just like getting jolted with electricity.

"I am sorry, Narada, I had not realised your presence just now"

"Please take a seat" gestured Sathya to the couch. Narada sat and she worshipped him and washed his feet, sprinkling water on head. She then asked, "What can I do in your service?"

"Oh nothing queen. I just came here because I want an answer to a question" said Narada.

"Hmm, if so, what is it, I will try to answer to the best of my knowledge" replied Satya.

"I want to know that Lord Krishna loves you or queen Rukmini more?" asked Narada

"What kind of question is this, sage? Of course, Krishna loves me more than Rukmini!"

"Are you sure?" inquired Narada doubtfully.

"Yes!"

"Then why don't we organize a competition to see who Lord Krishna loves more- is it you or Rukmini. What do you say?" asked Narada leading Sathya into a trap.

"Is it necessary to do this competition, I don't see the importance!" replied Sathya.

"It is necessary to know who is dearer to Lord Krishna." said Narada gently. Sathya kept quiet hearing this.

Seeing that Sathya's silence, "Or are you saying Rukmini is dearer to Krishna?" asked Narada to provoke her.

"Of course not!!" replied Sathya angrily recovering from her silence. She sighed.

"I agree to the competition but what is it?", asked Sathya curiously.

"It's simple. To show that Lord Krishna loves you more than anything we must request Krishna to sit on a weighing scale, then you must do whatever you can to make the scale balance."

"What kind of competition is this, Narada?", questioned Sathya.

"This competition will verify your statement that Krishna loves you more. If you succeed then the whole world will know that Krishna loves you more than Rukmini", replied Narada.

"That's all?" snorted Sathyabhama.

"But, if you can't, then Krishna has to follow me to the heavenly kingdoms."

"I will balance the scale in no time!", shouted Sathya.

"Let Rukmini know that she is nowhere near to my beauty", said Sathya strongly.

By chastising Rukmini in strong words, Sathyabhama prepared an enormous weighing scale at the hall of the palace. Narada smiled at her actions.

He said, "I am going to call Lord Krishna here and once He is here, the game begins".

"Yes, call Him" replied Satyabhama quickly. Narada nodded his head and disappeared from the sight and appeared in front of Krishna who was just laying on His bedstead.

Upon seeing the sage, Lord Krishna came down the bed, and requested Narada to sit on the bed. After paying respect to the Supreme Personality of Godhead, the great sage narrated the incidents between His wives. "I have known already regarding this.", said Krishna. Narada requested Krishna to sit on the weighing scale in order to remove the arrogance of Sathyabama.

"As long as you do not cause any trouble between My wives, I will follow whatever you plan to do", Krishna said.

"Don't worry, lord, I am doing this in order to curb Sathya's pride", replied Narada.

"Hmm, yes you are correct. Carry on with your play, I will just follow you, then" said Krishna gently.

"Then, we must go now", said Narada quickly. Krishna stood and vanished as does Narada.

Syamasundara and Narada appeared in front of Sathyabama. They also saw the citizens of Dvaraka (except Rukmini) were gathering there. Sathyabhama at once bowed to her husband and said in a highly pitched tone, "My lord, please sit on this scale"

"What is this, Sathya? What is the matter", asked Lord Krishna acting as if He doesn't know anything. Lord Krishna is the supreme actor. When He descends, he played perfectly as human being.

"I want to show Rukmini that I understand You more" replied Satyabhama.

"Hmm, if that is your wish, then ok", said Krishna climbing up the scale and sat.

Narada at once said, "My dear Sathyabama, you have exactly one hour to make this scale balance. If you fail, then Krishna must follow me to the heavenly bodies."

"This is an easy task, I will sure succeed," Sathyabama said loudly, in a confident manner.

"Then let's start," said Narada.

At once Sathyabama ordered her maid-servants which were numbered thousands, "All of you go and bring me pile of gold each, and be quick." The maid-servants immediately hurried and brought a pile of gold each.

"Quickly, put all the gold on this pan," she ordered. The maid-servants at once poured the gold on the pan. The amount of gold on the pan was like a small hill, but to Sathyabama's surprise, the scale is not even moved an inch. In other words, Krsna is still heavier than the pile of gold.

The audience gasped and questioned among themselves that a hill of gold is not enough to balance Krsna. Sathyabama grew anxious. As the time continues to run, she said in a loud voice, "Citizens of Dvaraka, please put all your jewelleries on this pan."

Requested by the queen, the citizens immediately put all their jewelleries on the pan. There are so much gold on the pan until the pile looked like a mountain.

But the enormous amount of the gold is not enough to balance the scales and Sri Krishna is still very much heavier. Narada laughed but stopped once Sathya threw a murderous look. Greatly flabbergasted by the weight of Krishna, Sathyabama said, "My dear

Narada, please give more time, so that I can find other materials to balance the scales"

"Sorry queen, this is the rule and do not forget that you accepted this. Please be quick as there is only half an hour left, or else Krishna must follow me," replied the sage.

Sathyabama sat down and cried. Krishna was enjoying this game but he kept quiet just to see the future actions of Sathyabama.

Seeing Sathyabama in lamentation, Narada himself approached her and said, "My dear queen, why don't you get help from Rukmini, she might be able to help."

Sathyabama looked up and replied, "My dear Narada, why should I call Rukmini, there is no way she can help, because she is inferior than me."

"Then, you made your decision, my queen. Krishna have to follow me to heaven," said Narada. Krishna hearing the statement of Sathyabama decided to bring the game furthur. Winking at Narada, Lord Krishna screamed, "Ahhh, help Me .... I am being pulled to the heaven!"

Anxiety flooded into Sathyabama's heart and she said quietly to one of her maid-servants, "Call upon Rukmini and tell her if she refuse to come then Krishna will be lost forever."

The maid-servant immediately went off to Rukmini's palace. Rukmini who was at that time reading the *Sama Veda*. She saw the maid servant of Sathya hurrying towards her. Feeling very curious, she asked "What is the matter?"

"Queen Rukmini, Lord Krishna is in trouble!"

"What are you talking about?!", screamed Rukmini. Her heart began to beat faster and faster.

"Yes, queen, queen Satyabhama had accepted the challenge from sage Narada. She needs to balance Lord Krishna on a weighing scale, but in spite of piles of gold, she failed."

"She requires your help!"

"I will come now!" screamed Rukmini but instead of following the servant, she rushed to the garden. "Queen! What are you doing?" asked the maid servant astonished.

"I need to find *tulasi* leaf", replied Rukmini. "What?" asked the maid. None of the queen's actions is making sense. How can she attempt to find a leaf in this situation.

"Ahh, I found it!" exclaimed Rukmini happily. She plucked the leaf and straightened her body.

"Lets go!", Rukmini yelled in anticipation and stormed to the hall followed by the maid servant.

Rukmini stepped into the palace. At once the audience began to move away, giving access to the queen. Rukmini walked passed them and she came to the center of the palace where she saw the scales- a black iron T with ropes linked to two golden dishes, each big enough to hold a person. She threw her glance to Lord Krishna who sat on one of the dishes, closing his eyes. Rukmini bowed to the great sage Narada. She walked to Sathyabhama who was on the floor looking half dead.

Rukmini said in a soothing motherly voice, "My dear Sathya, please don't cry. Krishna will not leave us, I promise."

Satya looked at Rukmini and replied, "It is my fault Krishna is in this situation. I want everyone to know that I love Him more than you". Rukmini kept silent for a moment, but she satisfied Satya with sweet words.

"Please Rukmini, please rectify my mistake", said Satyabhama choking back her tears.

"I will look into it, don't worry", answered Rukmini.

Rukmini walked towards the scale and placed the tulasi leaf on the pile of gold. Immediately, the scale tilted and the dish whereby Krishna is sitting began to rise and eventually it became exactly balanced with Him. The audience gasped and Narada smiled.

Sathyabama stopped crying suddenly. She walked slowly to Rukmini. "Rukmini, how *tulasi* leaf can do this miracle?", stammered Satyabhama. "*Tulasi* leaf is the most sacred plant in the universe as it is the dear most devotee of Krishna." answered Rukmini. Satyabhama kept silent after hearing Rukmini's answer.

Wiping her tears, she walked towards Krishna who was climbing down from the dish. She fall to His feet and said in deep remorse voice, "My lord, it was my fault that being envious of Rukmini. You are the original father of creation, please excuse my mistake. I know that you enacted this play just to curb my pride".

Lord Krishna who is very merciful to His devotee, raised Sathyabhama and embraced her. Wiping her tears with His fingers, Krishna said, "My dear Sathya you must know that I do not like My devotees to be proud, thinking that he or she is better than the others. If it happens, I will end the pride by some tactic" "I am the supreme master and thus I accept everyone's service. There is no need to be proud."

Sathya nodded her head in shame. "I am very sorry, Rukmini for underestimating you", she said slowly. Rukmini smiled and consoled her with sweet words. Krishna smiled when He saw His wives finally in peace.

The Supreme lord threw His arms each on Rukmini and Sathya and they walked back to their quarters. The great Narada smiled as he served his purpose in curbing Satya's pride and vanished.

NOTE:

This tale of Sathyabhama trying to balance Krishna with golds failed because Krishna is the Supreme Personality of Godhead. He is the resting place of entire universe, so how can an insignificant amount of gold can be equal to Him?. However, the *tulasi* leaf managed to balance the lord's weight, as *tulasi* is the topmost devotee of the lord. Krishna tells the world that His devotee is as much to respected and worshipped as He does.

The *tulasi* leaf is mandatory in worshipping Lord Vishnu and his incarnations. The *tulasi* is most powerful plant spiritually in the universe. If one holds a *tulasi* during the point of death, one will go to Vaikuntha planets.

LIBERATION OF HANUMAN; THE MONKEY GOD

Hanuman; the monkey-god is actually an incarnation of Lord Shiva. He was born in aim to assist Lord Rama's struggle against the demon lord; Ravana who was at the time terrorizing earth and every corner of this universe with his great powers.

It was told in Ramayana that Hanuman was born to a female ape by the name of Anjana. His father is Vayudeva (the wind deity). Apes in Hinduism are known as Vaanara. Hanuman is also known as Anjaneya Deva. It means that 'Son born to Anjana'. This is an interesting tale that happened after his birth.

Every morning after Hanuman wakes up from his sleep, his mother will feed him with fruits to appease his hunger, only then she will perform her morning prayers.

However, one day the fruit store in the house was exhausted. Anjana said to herself, "How am I going to feed Hanuman?". She turned her head and looked at Hanuman who was suckling his small finger while fast asleep on the mat.

Anjana sighed and suddenly she taught of one brilliant idea of going out and to collect the fruits before her son wakes up. Smiling to herself, she carried a woven basket and in no time stormed out of the house after kissing gently on Hanuman's forehead. He immediately writhed like a snake but continued sleeping as if nothing happened. Anjana left the house carrying the basket with her.

After a few hours, Hanuman opened his eyes. He woke up and in a flash he sat. Hanuman threw a sweeping glance around the wooden hut. His stomach started to rumble as if many people were beating drum inside his stomach. Hanuman clutched his stomach and exclaimed softly, "Ahhhh... I am so hungry!"

Hanuman decided that there is only one way to end this torment and agony. He needs Anjana. He called upon his mother loudly, "Mother!" "Mother!" cried Hanuman loudly. "Where are you?" "I am starving here!" continued Hanuman.

No answer. "Where is she?" he asked quietly and in a slightly annoyed tone. Hanuman stood and surveyed around his house. He suspected that his mother was playing some hide and seek game with him and he is not happy with her actions especially when his stomach is groaning for food.

"Oh my god!" "Where is she?" asked Hanuman weakly. He started to look around the house not only to find his mother but also to find some fruits which may be hidden, but no luck.

In the end Hanuman sat down, exhausted. He could neither find his mother nor any fruits. "Maybe, she is outside fending the garden," Hanuman exclaimed and in excitement, he ran out of the house screaming, "Mother!" repeatedly. As soon as he was out of the house, Hanuman caught the sight of the sun which was high up the sky and filling earth with warmness.

"Ah, what a large orange floating on the sky," Hanuman said clapping his hands and doing some sort of monkey dance. "Mother can wait, I am so hungry now! And I am going to eat that juicy orange," shouted Hanuman pointing his finger to the sun.

Without wasting a single moment, Hanuman rose to the sky and in a blink of an eye he flew towards the sun in great speed resembling a rocket. His mouth started to drool at the sight of the so-called orange. Hanuman acquired the flying ability because his father, Vayu is the wind god.

Within moments, Hanuman passed across the atmosphere of the Earth and sped towards the sun quickly. Hanuman extended both his hands as if were to catch the sun. He came near to the sun's surface when the monkey god saw an immense shape of a snake approaching. The snake was gigantic and its scales gleamed in the sunlight.

The snake opened its mouth which was big enough to swallow planets. The fangs glistened as it reflected the rays of the sun. Unfortunately, as it gets near to accomplish its mission, the snake which was known as Raghu saw a monkey speeding towards the same goal. "What is the Vaanara doing?" "Don't tell me he is also going to devour the sun", thought Raghu momentarily paralysed in space.

"Yes, he is going to eat the sun!" yelled Raghu speeding to meet Hanuman who did not realise the cosmic snake is rushing towards him.

Raghu roared as he lunged forward to attack Hanuman. No one dares to compete with him to devour the sun until now.

Hanuman was stupefied when he heard the roaring sound of Raghu. He turned his head just in time to see the fangs ready to sink into his flesh. As quick as wind, Hanuman dodged. Raghu turned its reptilian head to Hanuman who was floating behind him.

Hissing and in great anger, Raghu attempted to sink its fang on Hanuman again. But the Vayu's son clutched the fangs with his hands. Using it, Hanuman did a somersault and landed on Raghu's back. Raghu did not realise this and he turned his snake head in every direction attempting to find the nuisance monkey which is futile.

Hanuman used his legs to squeeze the snake's body and using his strong hands he strangled the snake. Raghu coughed and spluttered. His strength diminished quickly and he prayed to King Indra immediately to save him.

Indra was sitting at his throne and was enjoying the dance performance by the celestial dancers while sipping his usual Soma juice, when he received Raghu's prayers asking for help.

"Raghu is calling me. Something had happened", mumbled Indra.

Indra closed his eyes. Using his mystic vision, he saw that the serpent was being attacked by a Vaanara. He opened his eyes and rose from his throne, mumbled angrily to himself, "It is the order that Raghu needs to engulf the sun and eclipse must take place within the time." "I have no idea who is this Vaanara which is foolish enough to obstruct Raghu's duty."

Indra took a deep breath pausing. "The monkey must be taught a lesson," he continued with a sour face.

Indra extends his right hand and in a split of a nanosecond, a five foot long with zigzag at both ends but the handle which was made from pure gold at the middle appeared. Indra clutched it with his powerful hands. Without saying a word, the king of heaven stormed out of his halls carrying the thunderbolt.

He came to his albino elephant, Airvata and climbed over it. He yoked the reins and Airvata sped across the sky and within few moments he reached the site where the fighting was still going on.

Indra saw Raghu was now tied with ropes and Hanuman who was sitting on its body covered with gleaming scales, pummelling with his mountain like fists. With each blow that can break mountains, Raghu let out a scream that is piercing. The scream travelled in all directions and rattled the upper and lower planetary systems.

Without wasting any moment, Indra aimed the *Vajra* to Hanuman and hurled at the monkey with his full strength. Hanuman did not expect any attack as he was concentrating on beating Raghu. He neither noticed Indra nor his advancing thunderbolt. Only after hearing the *whissh* sound, Hanuman turned his head just in time to get struck with the *Vajra*. The thunderbolt injured his chin at the moment of impact and the *Vajra* like a boomerang flew back to Indra's clutches.

The injured Hanuman looked startled and petrified for a moment. He looked at Indra, whom he did not realise just now, smiled at the Lord of Devas and fall straight to earth like a meteor. Hanuman propelled downwards with the velocity no human can imagine. Within seconds, he landed with a loud thud, so explosive till it created a huge crater.

All of a sudden, the wind and air stopped moving. The air shimmered and the god of wind; Vayudeva appeared at the crater. Vayudeva stooped and picked up his child in his arms. He looked at the monkey god and his pupil dilated when the wind god saw Hanuman's chin was bleeding profusely. The blood dripped at Vayu's arm. This is also when Hanuman got his name as Hanu means jaw and Man means disfigured. It roughly means 'disfigured jaw'.

The wind god looked upon the sky and shouted, "Indra, how dare you injure my son with your Vajra. You will pay as I am going to withdrew all my air and wind!" pausing, Vayudeva closed his eyes and murmured.

After murmuring, Vayu walked towards a cave and followed by the personified forces of air. Vayu entered the cave, carrying his son with one hand and with other, he flicked his hand and the boulder rotates across and shut the entrance of the cave. In other words, the Lord of Wind withdrew all his forces into the cave. There is no air on earth as beings started to pass out to the death kingdom.

Indra who was sitting on his throne was feeling uneasy. "I can feel that beings are dying on Earth," he mumbled to himself. The king of heaven walked briskly leaving his halls. He called upon his mount again Airvata and together they travelled to earth.

Indra surveyed the earth as his feeling was correct. All beings, humans and animals began to gasp for air and then, they would collapse and die. Sakra realised quickly that there is no air force on Earth. He immediately traced Vayudeva using his mystic powers to a cave.

Indra asked Airvata to leave him at the cave entrance. The king passed through the boulder obstructing the cave's mouth with ease, just like a ghost passing through solid wall. He saw Vayudeva was sitting on the floor of the cave holding the Vanaara that Indra attacked just now. Feeling surprised, Indra walked hurriedly to Vayu.

"My dear Vayu, why have you stopped the air forces?, the organisms are dying" asked Indra, crouching. Vayu looked up at Indra's face with tears flowing down his cheeks. "It was you who injure my son and now he is unconscious due to your Vajra." "And now you want me to allow others to live?" shouted Vayu.

Indra was taken aback. So far Vayu had not spoken against him until now. "My dear Vayu, it was your son that attempted to eat the sun, so in order to prevent it, I had injured him with my thunderbolt," answered Indra gently.

"I will heal him," continued the king of heaven, placing his right hand on Hanuman's bleeding chin. A glow of light emanated from his hand and entered Hanuman's chin. Within seconds the bleeding stopped and the wound healed by itself. "From now, your son will be immune to *Vajra* and his body will become stronger than *Vajra*," blessed the king of heavens. Glow of red light appeared and entered Hanuman's body. Indra then disappeared.

After the entrance of the mysterious light, Hanuman suddenly opened his eyes and looked at his father, Vayudeva who was peering at his chin. "What happened, father?" asked Hanuman gently still lying on his father's lap. Vayu narrated the incidence that caused Hanuman's chin to be injured. Hanuman touched his chin with his left hand.

All of a sudden, the cave is illuminated with bright light, when the other gods started to appear headed by Lord Brahma and Lord Shiva. Upon the seeing the creator and the destroyer, Vayudeva stood up immediately after putting his son on the ground. "I offer my respectful obseicances to Sri Brahma and Sri Shiva," said Vayudeva folding his hands and bowing his head.

The two great gods and other gods blessed Vayudeva. Brahma turned and walked to Hanuman. He picked him up. With some twinkling of eyes, the creator said in a powerful voice, "Hanuman will be protected from any weapon in a war!" and a red glowing light emanated from Lord Brahma's hand and entered the monkey god's body. Brahma passed Hanuman to Mahadeva who held him and said, "You will live long and have scriptural wisdom and the ability to cross ocean."

It is said the gods knew about Hanuman's future and gave the boons accordingly. For example Lord Shiva probably knew that there will be time when Hanuman needs to cross some ocean. This is true because later in Ramayana, during the quest of finding Sita, Hanuman crosses the great Indian Ocean to the island of Lanka.

I am sure that without Shiva's boon, Hanuman will not be able to cross the ocean. Thus from my opinion, the gods actually knows Hanuman's fate and to help him, they gave him the boons which will come in handy later when he assist Lord Rama against Ravana.

Similarly of how the two gods blessed Hanuman, other gods also showered their blessings. Agnideva; the fire god blessed Hanuman with immunity to fire. This bleesings proved useful when Ravana instructed to light up Hanuman's tail in later part of Ramayana. Surya, the sun god gave him the knowledge of yogic siddhi called as mahima.

Bakthivendata Swami stated that mahima siddhi is a type of yogic perfection whereby one can expand as desired. This knowledge comes in handy whenever Hanuman wanted to expand himself into a large or small form.

Yama, the lord of death blessed him that death will not come to him. Thus, it is said that Hanuman is one of the immortals in the Hinduism.

By this way, Hanuman obtained many blessings from the gods. After obtaining these boons, Hanuman said to his father, "My dear father, please excuse me, mum would definitely will be finding me." Vayu embraced his son and replied, "Please return to your mother."

After taking his father's permission, the monkey lord rolled the boulder to the side, turned back just in time to see Vayudeva disappear leaving behind scent of breeze that swept Hanuman's face. Smiling to himself, Hanuman shot into the sky and made way to his mother's hut.

NOTE:

Hanuman is actually an aspect of Shiva known as Rudra. He is a top most devotee of Lord Rama. Hanuman's spiritual master is Surya (sun god). After obtaining the knowledge, Hanuman went on to serve under the monkey king, Sugreeva until Rama came.

LORD GANESHA - THE GREAT AUTHOR OF MAHABHARATA

The Hindu epic, Mahabharata tells us about the heroic feud of Pandavas against their cousins known as Kauravas. It ends in the climactic battle of Kurukshetra, one of the bloodiest wars that happened in India approximately 5000 years ago during the reign of Lord Krishna. The story of how Mahabharata was written is narrated here.

At the end of the third age of mankind, known as Dvapara Yuga, the great sage, Vedavyasa wanted to write a Hindu epic about the heroic Pandavas and the climactic battle of Kurukshetra in order to show humanity about how a virtuous person should live.

Vedavyasa asked himself, "Who will be worthy enough to write down my verses?" The sage thought for a long time but he cannot think of who is capable enough of doing the task. In the end, he decided to ask for an advice from Lord Shiva.

Vedavyasa disappeared from the sight and appeared at the entrance of Kailash Mountains. Upon paying respect to Nandisvara, who is the guardian of the entrance, the great sage entered.

He made a beeline to where the throne of Lord Shiva is located on the summit of Kailash. Upon reaching his destination, the sage saw that many devotees were prostrating before the three-eyed god and paying respects to him.

Shiva was in deep meditation. His eyes were closed and his chest was moving up and down slowly. The sage said, "O Lord Shiva, best among the Vaishnavas, please make time for me".

Upon hearing the words of Vedavyasa, Shiva opened his eyes slowly. He saw Vedavyasa and smiled at him. "What is your purpose of you coming to Kailash?"

"My dear Lord, I have thought of an epic about the heroic Pandavas and their struggle. But I require someone to write it down." Vyasa paused. "Please advise me".

Shiva smiled and replied, "Vedavyasa, I think Ganesha is the suitable candidate. He has supreme knowledge and is very intelligent. He definitely can help you."

Vedavyasa said thankfully, "If Lord Ganesha can help me in writing the epic; I request your permission to bring him back to earth to do the job".

"So be it," answered Shiva. He raised his right hand and called, "Ganesha, come here now."

In a blink of an eye, Ganesha appeared at the scene. He immediately paid respect to his father and the sage.

"What is your purpose, father for summoning me here? Please tell me and I shall carry out your wishes." said Ganesha respectfully.

"Vedavyasa said that he has an epic in his mind but he requires someone to put his words down so that people of earth can benefit from it" "I have personally recommended you to take this job."

"As you wish, father, I will carry out immediately." replied Ganesha

"Then, we must go now." interrupted Vyasa quickly.

Lord Ganesha nodded. The elephant god and Vyasa bowed to Lord Shiva. He blessed them and in a second, they disappeared from Kailash and appeared at the residence of Vedvyasa; hut surrounded by lush green forest and of different flowers blooming.

"So, Vyasa, please instruct me what to do," said Ganesha stroking his trunk in deep elephant voice.

Vyasa said with great respect, "My dear Vinayagar, please write down my verses that I will say."

"Then so be it," replied Ganesha pausing. "But, you must never hesitate or stop doing your job," cautioned Ganesha.

Upon hearing the words of Ganesha, Vedavyasa at once counter cautioned by saying, "If you say so, then you also must understand the verses that I composed before writing it down."

"If that is your wish, I agree to it. So, let us begin immediately," answered Ganesha. He sat on the concrete seat which was under a tree and folded his legs. Ganesha meditated a while and immediately a pot filled with blue ink and a feather appeared. Besides the ink pot, stacks of paper appeared in front of the lord of success. Vedavyasa took his seat a few metres from Ganesha, but facing him.

"Ok, please begin," instructed Ganesha holding the feather, ready to write. Vedavyasa drew his breath deeply and began to compose the verses of Mahabharata. Lord Ganesha immediately understood the verses and wrote it down.

Vedavyasa started composing more complex verses. These causes Lord Ganesha to take some time to understand them before writing. Thus, Vyasa brought time, to compose other verse in his mind and continued his verbal instructions without stopping.

The process of writing the Mahabharata took a long time, but in that period of time, neither Vedavyasa stopped in his job nor can't Lord Ganesha understand the verses.

Suddenly, "Oh! My pen is broken!" exclaimed the Lord. However, Vedavyasa ignored the god's statement and continued to compose the verses.

Ganesha on the other hand was in desperate situation, as his only writing tool failed him. Thinking speedily, Ganesha used his hand and hold the tusk. With a loud snap, he broke off his right tusk. Smiling to himself, he dipped the tusk in the ink and used it to write. Vyasa was astonished to see the lord gives so much sacrifice for wisdom. He even sacrificed his tusk to save the Mahabharata from ruination.

Lord Ganesha had demonstrated to the world that wisdom and education is very important. When pursuing studies, one must be ready to make sacrifices if necessary. We cannot expect education and wisdom is easy to obtain.

Ultimately, Vedavyasa finished composing the final verse of Mahabharata. Ganesha also finished writing the verse using his tusk.

"Lord, the Mahabharata is over." "It is ready to be presented to mankind." said Vyasa

"I am glad, Vyasa that this writing job is over and done" replied Ganesha breathing deeply.

"Lord, may I know the reason why you broke your tusk just in order to finish writing the Mahabharata?" asked Vedavyasa testily.

"Mahabharata portrays wisdom and my greatest priority is wisdom. No matter what ever obstacles appear when I am doing my intellectual job, I will sacrifice whatever it takes"

"Wisdom is the most important in one's life and no one should give up in obtaining knowledge"

"If one gives up in chasing knowledge, one is as foolish as lower animals". "Obstacles will appear in anyone's path. It is the nature. No one can be freed from obstacles. But making it as a reason not to achieve something in life is certainly not appropriate." explained Ganesha

"My Lord if obstacles appear in one's life, what should be done?" questioned Vedavyasa.

"My dear sage, before starting any job be it studies or others, the person must think of me in his heart and he need to say '*Om Gum Ganapathiye Namaha*'. As soon he think of me and chant my *mantra*, I will remove his obstacles and make him succeed in his job."

This is the reason that when a person wants to take some task, he must pray to Lord Ganesha so that his job will be much easier and success is assured.

"Thank you my Lord. You have not only helped me writing the Mahabharata but also had showered me with some solutions", said Vyasa bowing and touching Lord Ganesha's feet. "The world will remember your deed of writing the Mahabharata." said Vedavyasa.

Lord Ganesha smiled and vanished. Vedavyasa also walked back to his hut.

Thus, the epic Mahabharata was presented to mankind and this tale tells us one of the reasons why Lord Ganesha's tusk was broken.

NOTE:

Vyasadeva is deemed to be the literary incarnation of Lord Vishnu. He is also one of the greatest sages because he explained Vedic knowledge in different ways to mankind. He is also the author of the *Srimad- Bhagavatam*

THE DELIVERANCE OF THE MOON GOD

The Hindus celebrate the birthday of Lord Ganesha which is known as the 'Vinayaka Chathurthi' or the 'Ganesha Chathurthi'. This day usually falls in the month of August or September each year. The birthday of Lord Ganesha is celebrated when he is revived by his father after the battle. The Hindus believe on that day, one is not allowed to look upon the moon because the moon god is cursed by Lord Ganesha. The tale is narrated here.

At the beginning of time, on Vinayaka Chathurthi, Lord Ganesha was sitting in his abode in the Kailash mountain, as usual munching his favourite food; the modhaka. He was flipping the *Rig Veda* as he munched the delicacy one by one and until finished. Vinayaka did not realize this and attempted to grab another without looking at the tray which is empty. When he failed to grab which is nothing but only air, Ganesha put down the *Veda* and peered at the tray.

"Hmmm, I have eaten everything and now it is finished." mumbled Ganesha. "And I am still hungry" continued the lord. Ganesha stroked his chin with his left hand, thinking hard.

"Ahh, I know, I shall go to earth and visit my devotees. I am sure that they have prepared a lot of modhaka for me," exclaimed Ganesha snapping his finger.

"Mother, I am going to earth to visit my devotees!," Vinayaka shouted at the top of his voice hoping that Parvathi who was at her quarters, listened to him.

Parvathi who was meditating, opened her eyes slowly. She sighed as her meditation is disturbed by Ganesha's piercing voice.

Parvathi stood and walked towards her son who was now sitting on the couch and practising his reciting of the *Vedas*. "Ganesha, why are you shouting to get my attention?" "It is very inappropriate to shout at your mother, even you wanted to ask something," scolded Parvathi.

"Sorry mother, I am too hungry to walk to your chambers", said Ganesha remorsefully.

"Ahh, I see that you have finished the modhaka in no time, you naughty boy," said Parvathi in slightly surprised tone. She wondered how he is able to eat all the modhaka in an eye blink.

"Never mind, Ganesha, I will ask the attendants to cook some more," suggested Parvathi taking a seat beside her son and threw her arms around the elephant god's shoulder.

"Its ok mum, I have decided to visit my devotees on Earth. Besides obtaining some food, in exchange I would bless them," replied Ganesha.

"Hmm, I think it is a splendid idea," replied Parvathi kissing her son's forehead. "You should go now, your birthday is coming to an end" continue Parvathi standing up and exited from the house to see her gardens.

"Yes, mum. I will go now," answered Ganesha softly and followed his mum outside. Ganaphati narrowed his eyes and surveyed the compounds looking for his mount which is a mouse. "Muushiga!!" Come here!", yelled Ganesha.

The mouse which was nibbling at the remnants of some plants in the garden, at once perked up its hairy ear after hearing its name being called by its master. The mouse at once put down the plant and rushed to Ganesha. It ran so fast, leaving behind the spiralling sand in its wake.

The mouse screeched to a halt in front of the elephant god. Ganesha immediately mounted mouse and yoked the reins. The mouse ran and suddenly took off exactly like a normal day aeroplane which would take off from a ramp.

Ganesha manuovered his mouse dodging some asteroids and meteors in the space. He directed his mouse to planet earth. Reaching the earthly planet in a split second, Lord Ganesha made way to a devotee's hut.

When the devotee saw Easenputra standing in front of his house, he immediately fell at the Lord's feet and offered respects. He invited Lord Ganesha to his house.

Lord Ganesha smiled and entered the house which was not very well furnished. However, the devotee offered mattresses which was made out of straw and said, "My lord, please sit down." Lord Ganesh did not want to refuse his devotee's need. "Umm, sure...... but I need to visit another devotee so I will just spend a little while," replied Ganapathi to the man as he sat on the mattress. The man nodded. "Please excuse me a while, I will bring some fruits", said the man.

"Ok, but please hurry", replied Ganesha. The man bowed and disappeared to the kitchen. Lord Ganesha swept a glance across the hut and saw that his statue which was decorated with garments and a pile of modhaka is laid at the statue's feet.

Lord Ganesha walked to his statue and immediately inhaled all the modhaka just like a vacuum cleaner. In no time, the tray is empty. Feeling satisfied the god blessed the devotee and vanished suddenly to another devotee's house.

"My lord, here is .....," said the man while walking and carrying a tray of fruits. He could not see Ganesha. The devotee frantically called, "Ganaphati! Vinayaka!" while running across the house but Ganesha is nowhere to be found. Suddenly, the devotee caught the sight of the empty tray. He smiled and silently prayed for the lord of the success blessing.

After visiting many of his devotees' house, Lord Ganesha had eaten a lot of modhaka in each and every devotee's house.

Lord Ganesha then whispered to himself. "Ok, I am full now but there is a lot of modhaka here," Ganesha glanced at the pile of modhaka which he collected from all the devotees' houses.

"I cannot eat anymore but I will take it to Kailash and eat it," thought the elephant god. He stooped and picked up the modhakas one by one. Lord Ganesha closed his eyes and murmured. All of a sudden a transparent sac appeared.

Lord Ganesh placed all the modhaka into the transparent sac as fast as a lightning. After the last modhaka, the lord stared at the sac. The sac immediately tied the knot by itself. Ganesh swung the sac on his shoulder exactly like how a schoolboy was to carry the backpack.

"Pfffttt!" whistled Lord Ganesha. The mouse which was nibbling at the roots of some vegetation at once perked up its furry ears and at once stopped chewing and thundered towards the lord.

Ganesha turned his elephant head when he hears the loud sound of his mouse. The mouse halted abruptly in front of the lord just like a racing car was applied of brakes.

Smiling, the god sat on the mouse flinging the modhaka filled sac and exclaimed, "Muushiga please return to Kailash, it is getting dark." The mouse understood and ran across the earthly sand.

A snake which was sleeping at a bush nearby felt disturbed due to the thundering noise. It opened its reptilian eyes and said annoyingly, "I will go and see what this noise all about is."

The reptile slithers out from the bush and saw a mouse running. It also saw Lord Ganesha on the mouse. Suddenly a mischievous plan began to bubble from the snake's mind. Grinning to itself, it decided to surprise the mouse.

When Muushiga began to cross the area, the snake suddenly sprang from the bush. The mouse let out a mousey scream and sped in opposite direction quickly.

In the astonishing speed, Lord Ganesha flew from his mount and landed on a tree branch. The branch of the tree could not withstand the god's weight and it broke, causing Ganesha to fall. He hit the ground with a loud thud. This creates a minor earthquake and the branches of the tree started to fall on the lord's head one after another. Ganesh breathed deeply and swept a glance. His mouse is missing in action.

'Great', thought the lord, slowly getting up and began sweeping the branches and leaves from his head. "Where is my modhaka?" asked Ganesh loudly to himself. He narrowed his eyes and caught the sight of his transparent sac which was lying beside a rock few miles away. The sac was ripped open and the contents were strewn out on the ground.

Ganesha groaned in total frustration seeing that all the modhaka get contaminated. He crashed on the ground lamenting.

During this incident, the moon which is known as Chandra was witnessing the incident from the night sky. The moon found that the incident of the mouse getting scared of a serpent and subsequently sending Ganesha to a tree is too funny. Unable to suppress his emotions, the moon cackled with laughter.

The laughter of Chandra travelled across the atmosphere and reaching Ganesha's enormous elephant ears. Ganesha stood and narrowed his eyes to find the source of the laughter. Anger flooded through his heart when he saw the moon laughing loudly at him.

Ganesha in great rage broke one of his tusks with his bare hands. The tusk broke with a loud sound resembling a thunderbolt of Indra striking the mountain. With full force and fuelled with anger, the son of Lord Shiva hurled the tusk towards the moon.

Chandra saw the tusk made way towards him and in a moment, it injured the moon extensively. In other words, the surface of the moon which was originally smooth and shiny now turned to be full of craters due to the tusk. As the moon is Chandra, and when the moon is injured, Chandra's face suddenly overgrown with blisters.

Lord Ganesha spoke angrily, "Chandra, you think it is funny that when a person met with an accident?!" pointing his index finger to the moon.

"Well, for your mistake of laughing instead of offering help, I strongly curse you; Chandra. You will wax for fifteen days and wane for another fifteen days!" Ganesha paused before continuing, "Anyone who would look at you during my birthday will suffer from terrible stomach ache!"

"Lord, I have made a mistake of laughing at you. Now I have realized it because your lordship had taught me a good lesson," said Chandra gloomily.

"I will not laugh anyone in trouble. Please deliver me from your curse," pleaded the moon when he saw Ganesha keeping silent.

Ganesha took a deep breath and after hearing the moon's pleas, the elephant god said gentle voice, "Since you have accepted your mistake, any unfortunate soul who looks at you during Vinayagar Chaturthi need to break seven coconuts in my temple in order to get relieved from the stomach ache."

Chandra bowed to Ganesh and returned to his abode, Chandraloka. Ganesh called upon his mouse and he too returned to Kailash Mountains.

So, don't attempt to gaze at the moon on Vinayaka Chathurthi!

NOTE:

Never ever should a person laugh when one is in trouble. We must offer help even if the person is an enemy. Lord Ganesha set the example that when a person fails to help and ridicule the helpless people, he will punish them. Thus, when you are able, you always must render help to others.

THE BIRTH TALE OF MARUTS-THE STORM GODS

Not many people knew the existence of the Maruts'- the storm gods. Existing in a group, the Maruts' were the attendants of King Indra in his heavenly court. They were a collective gods, however even the scriptures cannot determine their exact numbers. The most trustable number is given in *Rig Veda* that states Maruts were countable to exact figure of 49. Some says they were 27 deities and some says they were 60. *Rig Veda* also gives another figure of 108. Thus, no one knows the exact figure of these storm gods. Here is the tale of how these storms gods came to being.

One of the mind sons of Lord Brahma is Marichi and he has a son by the name of Kashyapa. Kashyapa grew to become one of the greatest sages in history. He is also one of the *saptarishi* (seven sages). Sage Kashyapa married the twenty three daughters of Prajapati Daksha (another mind son of Brahma). Two of Kashyapa's wives are Aditi and Diti.

Aditi and Diti were sisters but enemies. Aditi's off springs were called as adityas' (gods) while the off springs of Diti were known as Daityas' (demons). As the time dawns, demigods and demons often wage war. This is due to demons always wanted to go against the laws of god. Bhaktivedanta Swami said that demons are always afraid of gods. Gods tried to protect the laws from the demons.

The gods are headed by Lord Indra (king of heaven) often wages war against the demons. In one account similarly Indra slew Diti's wicked children. This caused Diti to be very angry towards the king of the heavenly kingdoms.

As she burned in the fire of anger, Diti said loudly to herself, "This useless king of heaven is getting on my nerves. Every time I bore a child he will kill them." "I will not tolerate this obnoxious act anymore! I will meet Indra myself." continued the mother of demons with such anger. She closed her eyes and murmured some words. In a blinding flash, she vanished.

Diti suddenly appeared at the gates of the heavenly kingdom which was guarded by Airvata. She waved her hand and suddenly the albino elephant moved aside and bowed to Diti giving her access through the gates.

Grinning to herself, she walked through the gate and made way to Indra's throne room. In a moment, she appeared in front of Indra throne room. She saw that Indra happily was sipping his Soma juice and enjoying the dancers by the celestial dancers.

Diti stormed across the hall and at the sight of the witch, the other gods sitting at their respective places grew anxious. The dancers fled in fear but Indra continued to sip his juice clearly not afraid. Diti stopped abruptly and suddenly clapped her hands loudly.

"Hmm, after you butchered my children, you enjoying your life" asked Diti loudly, pointing her index finger decorated with a miniature human skull ring to Sakra.

Indra kept silent. Diti fumed at Indra who is not afraid at the sight of her.

"So you think you are powerful?" asked Diti in her dangerously calm voice.

"I am the most powerful of the gods", Indra gloated steadying himself. Suddenly a lightning bolt appeared in his hands which emitted power beyond human speculation.

"I see that you are drunken with pride", said Diti eyeing the thunderbolt from the corner of her eyes. Diti said suddenly loudly, "Listen here Indra; I will conceive a child, whom I promise you will not be able to kill. Then, lets' see whether you still have your pride or not."

"Whatever you say, Diti you cannot overcome me, if any of your children came forth and challenge the gods, I shall destroy them", replied Indra confidently.

Saying that he threw his thunderbolt. The thunderbolt passed through the roof of the hall like an image. It suddenly propelled downwards making its way to a mountain. Once it reached the mountain, the peak of the mountain were completely shaved off and it fall with a great sound that shook the earth.

Diti smiled and the smile suddenly turned into uproar of laughter as if the whole incident of shaving the peak of the mountain is a piece of joke.

"Why are you laughing, are you not afraid?" asked Indra arching his thick eyebrows. "Afraid? Me? Foolish king, do you expect that your mere action of destroying a mountain will frighten me?" yelled Diti.

"No Indra, you thought wrong and now you will witness my power as this time my child become more powerful than you and you will beg me for forgiveness which clearly you won't get", continued the demoniac mother. She suddenly waved her finger to Indra, warning him and in a flash of light disappeared.

Indra grew anxious hearing Diti's warning and whispered, "Whatever happens, the children Diti must be destroyed and cannot be more powerful than me." "I must find out what is Diti's plan."

Diti; a sorceress came to her hut and said to herself, "I will practice tapas aided by my magic for hundred years; I will give birth to a son that will be more powerful than Indra himself."

With that vow, she practiced austery aided by her black magic. But before she started her tapas, she drew a circle with a white chalk. Then Diti entered within the circle, closed her eyes and started her act of black magic.

Up in the heavens, Indra sensed that something is wrong. He called, "Vayudeva, come here at once!" Vayu appeared in front of Indra and bowed. He asked, "What is the matter, why have you summoned me here?" "I want you to go to Diti's hut and observe her." said Indra in a commanding tone.

Vayu bowed and disappeared. He observed Diti using his mystic power. He saw that the witch was sitting in a circle and murmuring something. Vayu said to himself, "What exactly is she doing? Let me wait and observe her some more".

The wind god continued observing Diti for quite some time. He saw Diti came out of her hut at dawn and entered the circle. Then she will close her eyes and murmur something until dusk. Once the sun sets in the west, she would wash her legs and enter her hut. This is her routine that goes on and on. However, on each day her stomach begin to bulge slowly like a balloon

"Ok, the time is up, I need to inform to Indra." said Vayu, appearing at the hall of heaven. Indra who was at that time listening to Brihaspati's teaching regarding the secrets of the universe, immediately raised his hand signalling Brihaspati to stop.

"Well, Vayu, what is Diti up to?" asked Indra enthusiastically. "She will enter a circle at dawn and will murmur something until dusk and then she will go to bed", answered Vayu. "That's it?" enquired Devendra.

"No"

"What's more?" asked Indra

Vayu continued, "And I also saw that her stomach is bulging and it increases day by day". Indra exchanged looks with Brihaspati.

"Ok, this is surprising" Indra mumbled to himself.

"Her children is forming", said Brihaspati softly. "Yes Indra, You must destroy the foetus while it still in the womb", suggested Vayu seriously. Indra nodded.

"I shall destroy her penance now", Indra replied and he rose with his hands holding thunderbolt. He disappeared from his throne room and suddenly appeared at Diti's hut.

There he saw a chalk drawn circle and Diti is sitting inside the circle with her eyes closed. Her stomach seems to bulge. Just like Vayu described. Indra hid behind a bush and hurled his weapon with power.

Suddenly, the transparent shield emerges from the circle like a bubble, causing *Vajra* to bounce off harmlessly. Diti still continued her meditations as if nothing happened. Indra was utterly surprised. His mouth was struck in an, 'O' shape for a moment. He caught the *Vajra* and returned to Amaravati with frustration.

"What happened?" asked Brihaspati who was waiting for Indra at the throne room. "Diti is protected by some sort of shield." "My *Vajra* has no effect on her", continued Indra slumping on his throne.

"Hmm, I see", said Brihaspati thoughtfully rubbing his silver coloured beard. Indra poured Soma juice from a jug into his glass and gulped it.

"How to kill the foetus?" Indra asked, wiping his mouth with his arm.

"You must keep an eye on Diti for these hundred years that when she mistakenly did not follow the rules of penance, that is when she is vulnerable and it is the time you will kill her child," suggested the advisor. "It is the only way."

"If she did not break the rules?"

"We must hope she does."

"I shall watch Diti carefully from now," replied Indra feeling determined.

Thus, the king of heaven watched Diti carefully for many years. But Diti is very careful and she does not break any rules.

The end of her penance is fast approaching. On the ninety-ninth year, Indra grew anxious as Diti did not break any rules and her stomach expands beyond anything.

"Diti is too careful about her penance." murmured Indra. "I have no choice than to ask for help", he said to himself.

He silently prayed to Lord Vishnu for help. "O Supreme Personality of Godhead, please help me to slay Diti's child."

Lord Vishnu who was lying on His snake received Indra's prayers. Smiling to Himself, the great lord used His mystic powers and caused Diti to lose her memory regarding the rules of penance.

As we know Lord Vishnu as Supersoul entered the beings heart. The *Bhagavad-Gita* says that: I am seated in everyone's heart and from Me come remembrance, knowledge and forgetfulness.

It is a rule that after practicing some arts, one must wash their legs before going to bed. However, this time, Diti forgot to wash her legs before bed.

Thus, her penance of practicing dark arts for all these years was futile. Diti once laid down to sleep, immediately remembered that she had forgotten to wash her legs.

"Oh shit!" she exclaimed, rising from her bed. She quickly went out of her hut to strengthen her protective circle with other methods, when at that moment she saw the whole dark sky immediately lit up just like billion of lamps.

"Oh my god!!!" screamed Diti as she saw the thunderbolt of Indra rushed towards her. She attempted to run and hide in her hut, but with her heavy bulging stomach made the escape plan impossible. Nothing she can do and she sank to ground, bracing herself to meet the death.

Vajra reached her and gored through her stomach, separating her body into two portions; the upper and lower portion. Her stomach was ripped open and the fully formed foetus dropped on the ground still being enclosed in the amniotic sac. The foetus was curled in the sac, the skin of the colour of pure gold. The eyes were closed but it scowled as if wanted to burst open the sac and jump out.

Indra appeared to see Diti's mangled body when he caught the sight of the foetus writhing inside the membrane like a python. The king of heaven walked slowly to the sac and with great care, gripping his *Vajra*.

He came in front of the foetus and saw that it had fully formed. Without wasting time, Indra used his mystic power to rip open the amniotic sac hoping to kill the foetus. The fluid flowed to the ground straight from the sac. The foetus followed the flow and came out of the sac. As soon as the product of Diti's conception is out, the sac disintegrated.

Indra's heart beat faster and faster as he crouched to take a closer look at the baby who appeared to be sleeping. Suddenly it opened its fearsome eyes causing Indra to stumble backwards in shock. Its eyes were flaming red exactly like every drop of blood is squeezed into the eyeball.

The baby which is a male suddenly showed his teeth to Indra and the king of the heaven saw that the baby has teeth made of steel which gleamed in the moonlight. Indra stood inspecting his new foe, his heart beating in worry.

The baby opened his mouth and let out a piercing cry. Indra closed his ears with his hands unable to stand the scream. He saw the mountains began to sway and wind started to howl.

Suddenly, there was blinding lights everywhere when the other gods appeared. Vayudeva spoke, "Indra, I think you must kill this child, it is dangerous." The others nod their head enthusiastically.

"I know," said Indra gritting his teeth. Indra threw his thunderbolt at the baby. Due to Vajra's impact, the baby separated into seven parts. However, each part began to regenerate as a whole individual.

Now there are seven babies with flaming eyes and steel teeth. All seven of them cried. Thus, the storm and earthquakes worsen. The gods looked surprised. Something beyond their knowledge has appeared.

Indra gasped and he aimed his thunderbolt to the baby precisely. With anger he hurled the weapon. The thunderbolt shook the world as Indra attacked all the seven babies. Similarly each of the babies separated into another seven babies. So, now there are forty-nine babies with the same characteristics. Their cries were unbearable.

"This is beyond our capacity" said Brihaspati thoughtfully.

"Let's ask Lord Vishnu", suggested Indra still looking at the forty-nine babies now started to crawl. One of them started uprooting a nearby tree and threw it twenty metres away.

Without any moment to lose as the situation is out of hand, the gods closed their eyes and offered sincere prayers to the Supreme Personality of Godhead. In a split second, Vishnu appeared. "Hmmm, I see that Diti's babies are making quite a nuisance here", said Vishnu.

"Yes, Lord, the babies are multiplying once struck with my weapon", complained Indra. Vishnu smiled and replied, "If that is the case, you should not attempt to kill the babies"

"If so, they will destroy the world; their cries alone cause earthquakes and hailstorms"

"Indra, you must not act harshly, these babies will be your attendants" answered Lord Vishnu petting one of the baby's head.

"But….. How is that even possible, these are children of Diti", stammered Indra.

"Take my word, Indra. These babies are nothing but an aspect of Lord Shiva, actually known as Rudra. Thus, these babies are the plenary portion of Lord Shiva although they are born from Diti."

After hearing the words from Lord Vishnu, that these babies were an aspect of Shiva gave Indra a splitting headache. Nevertheless, he nodded.

Lord Vishnu said, "Since they are an aspect of Rudra, it is their nature to be aggressive. Let them be named as Maruts".

Saying so, Lord Vishnu blessed the forty-nine babies and vanished.

So, the forty-nine foetuses grew up and surprisingly short time. They serve Indra and whenever Indra wanted to cause storm, he will instruct them and the Maruts will do his bidding. The *Rig Veda* further states that the Maruts wore golden helmets and breastplates. They were armed with axes used to split clouds so that rain could fall. The Maruts were capable of shaking the mountains and destroying forests. These storm gods were very violent and aggressive holding lightning and thunderbolts, roaring like lions, they ride golden chariots drawn by ruddy horses. It is rumoured that the Maruts can be found in the northern parts of the world. They are gods of violence and destruction, so do not attempt to look for them!

NOTE:

The name Maruts came from the word, *Marod-ih* meaning 'Don't cry'. These storm gods are also known as Marutas or Marutgana.

THE SMASHING OF LORD KUBERA'S PRIDE

Once upon a time, Kubera who was the treasurer of the gods grew very proud of his wealth. He thought to himself, "My material opulence is of no limit. I want to organize a feast to celebrate my great opulence"

"Let me invite every gods and celestial beings to my feast and let them feel astounded at the sight of my riches", thought Kubera cackling with laughter.

Kubera thus began sending his invitations to every god he could lay eyes upon. Finally he set eyes upon Lord Shiva. Kubera thought that since Shiva is very poor so much so that he could not construct his own house while meditating and he was not even clothed properly, this is a great opportunity to humiliate the lord. Kubera mistakenly thought that Mahadeva was not eligible for the rank of 'Greatest demigod' since he was materially not very opulent.

Grinning to himself, the king of Yakshas at once yoked his vehicle, the *pusphaka vimana* and made his way to Kailash to invite him to the feast. In reality, Kubera wanted to humiliate Shiva.

The thought of Kubera about Lord Shiva is not correct. Shiva is the master of this material universe. Everything in this material universe is actually under him.

Kubera parked his *pushpaka vimana* at the entrance of Kailash great golden gates. He jumped down and his eyes surveyed the surroundings of the snow mountain.

Inhaling the cold air which is lethal to any mortals, Kubera walked past the gate which was guarded by the ghanas as usual "Welcome to Kailash, Lord Kubera, your presence had certainly light up this place," spoke one of the ghana bowing.

Upon hearing the words, Kubera replied in loud and sarcastic tone, "All of you ghanas, are not eligible to be with Shiva, look at you ..." pointing his index finger to a fat ghana whose stomach is bulging out as if he is pregnant for few months. "You are so fat and not even clothed!" Kubera chided and walked quickly. The ghanas look upon each other confused.

Kubera reached Lord Shiva's meditation place in an eye blink. He saw the great three eyed god sitting and meditating with eyes closed. His great strong chest move up and down in a beautiful rhythmic motion. Golden aura emanates from him temporarily blinds Kubera.

Kubera bowed until his golden crown bedecked with jewel touched the ground of snow. Lord Shiva sensed his devotee's presence and opened his eyes slowly. He said, "Kubera, all glory to you, what is the purpose you came to Kailash?"

Kubera rose but with folded hands he requested humbly, "My dear Lord Shiva, the greatest of all, I have prepared a magnificent feast at my place, my humble request is you must attend this feast"

Shiva sensed that the speech of Kubera is of a sarcastic tone. He immediately understood that inviting him to the feast is actually an attempt to humiliate him. Realising this, Shiva smiled and replied, "It is so nice of you to invite me, but unfortunately, I could not make it as I need to help Parvati in her performance"

Hearing this statement, Kubera's face morphed pitifully. "Nevertheless, in order to satisfy you, I will send my son to your feast." continued Lord Shiva after observing Kubera's face.

Kubera snorted and thought to himself, 'I wanted you to attend to get humiliated but now you wanted to send your son.' Shiva clearly understood his devotee pride. Nevertheless, he smiled and simultaneously raised his right hand and in an act of blessing called, "Vinayaka, please come here."

In a flash, Ganesha appeared with folded hands. He immediately bowed to his father and turned his head to bow to Kubera. Lord Ganesha spoke, "My dear father, why you summoned me?"

"Vinayaka, listen here carefully, Kubera had organised a feast. He invited me to attend but ah..." Lord Shiva paused. "I have more pressing things at the moment, so I can't make it and you, must take over my place."

Ganesha widened his pupils and glanced at Kubera who looked not at all pleased and then he shot a look at his father. Lord Shiva twinkled his eyes quickly. Ganesha smiled when he fully understood the situation. His father actually wanted him to teach a lesson to Kubera.

"Yes father, I will go to the feast," answered Vinayaka flapping his elephant ears back and forth like some sort of enormous fan.

"Lord, are you absolutely sure that Ganesha can eat. He is a small child and I don't think that he could even finish the portion given to him," said Kubera sarcastically.

Lord Shiva laughed loudly as if Kubera had made a great joke. The three eyed god's laughter was so loud until it created an avalanche in the distant mountains of Kailash.

"Kubera, you don't know Vinayaka's appetite, he has huge appetite and I hope that you will provide enough food for him. I must warn you, if you fail to give enough food, he will wreak chaos. So be cautious," warned Shiva.

"Don't worry lord, I will make sure that your son obtains enough food," boasted Kubera. He turned to Ganesha who was standing like an ice statue observing the conversation between his father and Kubera.

Vinayaka told himself, "Kubera's pride had taken over his mind, he is clouded with it and I must prevent this."

"Kubera, can we go now?" asked Vinayaka patting his bulging stomach like a drum. "Oh, sure," answered Kubera. Both gods took their permission from Lord Shiva and in a blink of an eye, they vanished. Lord Shiva fell into his world of meditation.

Vinayaka and Kubera appeared at Kailash entrance. They exited the golden gates which was guarded by the ghanas and made way to the magnificent *pusphaka vimana*. Without talking to each other, the gods climbed the chariot and Kubera yoked the reins. The *pusphaka vimana* rose to the sky and in a split of a second, vanished from atmosphere.

Within few minutes, they reached the outskrits of Kubera's capital city which is located in Ahalya at the Himalayan Mountains.

The chariot descended and landed amidst of many people sending dust upwards.

Kubera and Ganesha climbed down. Kubera started to boast about the magnificent gardens to Vinayaka, who looked not at all interested. Finally, Ganesha snorted and said in annoying voice, "Kubera, let's go to the dining hall. I am starving here."

"Oh, I am sorry let's go," answered the king of Yakshas, taking lead into the palace halls, gesturing Shiva's son to follow his lead.

Once they are in the dining hall which was decorated vibrantly with hanging chandelier and numerous pictures depicting Kubera in various deeds. The dining table was so large until it could accommodate thousands of guests. Foods of each kind were piled up like mountains.

Ganesha smacked his lips as he saw other gods were eating the *halava* and some others were munching on various foods. Without wasting any moment, Ganapathi walked briskly to one of the empty seat and crashed on it.

He extends both of his arms and pulled a nearby lying tray which was laden with grapes and oranges. Ganesha inhaled the fruits like a vacuum cleaner and in an astonishing moment, the tray is empty. Everyone at the feast turned to look at him in great admiration and surprise. Kubera narrowed his eyes.

The elephant headed god ignored the surprised gaze of the guests, but he set his eyes upon another tray full of *palkova*. This time the tray is a bit far from his reach. Ganesha moved his trunk and the trunk like an air sucker sucked the *palkova* one by one till all of them are finished.

This is not the end for the mighty Ganesha, for he vowed to teach Kubera a lesson. Ganapathi ferociously ate each and every food on the table, not leaving even one of them for the guests.

The guests were left looking upon each other dismayed faces and simultaneously turned their head slowly upon Ganesha who was busy munching the *rasagula* at the moment.

Kubera at once understood that Ganesha wanted to curb his pride. At once, the god of the wealth ran to Ganesha, and with folded hands, began to offer his apology, "My dear Ganapathi, I have foolishly overestimated my amount of wealth and clearly it had clouded my mind and senses."

The statement of Kubera is correct. According to the great philosopher; Bhaktivedanta Swami in his book entitled Krsna, he explained that material opulence can be elevating or degrading. If a person were to attach very much to the opulence, his life would be degraded as material riches have done to Kubera. Even though Kubera is a god but yet he is still clouded with material wealth. Thus in order to save him, Ganesha needs to enact this play.

Ganesha however ignored Kubera's prayers but asked him, "Kubera, is this you have? I thought you said great feast, and what a pity, the food here are so little and yet you brag in front of my father!"

"I need more food!" boomed Ganapathi and he banged the table.

The table tilled towards him and causes the plates, cups and rays to fall towards Ganesha. The elephant god opened his mouth and in few seconds his mouth seems to enlarge. The plates and others all dropped into his mouth. Successfully, keeping the plates and others in his mouth, Ganesha gulped all of these in a single go. The act of Ganesha was the last straw for the guests. They ran pushing each other and disappearing in a flash. Only Kubera stood with his folded hands and trembling body.

Kubera looked frightened and pleaded, "Lord, I have made a grave mistake, please forgive me."

Ganesha said in a mocking tone, "Kubera, what a pitiful disgrace to me. I thought there is more food."

"Lord, all the food is finished and there is none" replied Kubera trembling.

"Then, I shall eat all your decorations," exclaimed Ganapathi happily. Without hearing Kubera's protests, he pushed his chair and walked to the nearby picture depicting a waterfall. Ganesha tore the picture from the wall and broke it into smaller pieces. Like crackers, he began to stuff the canvas into his mouth.

Finished eating the picture, Lord Ganesha made way to the next decoration and began to eat it too. Kubera was so afraid that Ganesha might eat him too. This of course is not at all possible but when fear takes over the mind it creates a situation whereby what is impossible seems to be possible.

Fear is only the illusory state created by mind. Mind is compared to a hurricane. To control a hurricane is very difficult; similarly to control the mind is just as difficult as it. If a person fails to control the mind, he will become the victim of the illusion created by the mind.

Feeling extremely afraid, the king of Yakshas prayed to Lord Shiva, "Lord, please come and stop your son from wreaking havoc.

I am very sorry to boast about my riches and now I realise my mistake" "Please Lord, please help me."

Shiva, who was meditating, opened his eyes as he sensed Kubera's prayers. Smiling, he at once vanished and appeared at Kubera's place. The lord saw Ganesha has eaten everything in the hall and he is now trying to eat the expensive curtains. Kubera however was still praying to him, unaware that Shiva is already there.

Seeing all of these, Lord Shiva felt funny. However the god said in a commanding tone "Ganesha, it's enough, come here at once!"

Ganesh stopped abruptly and let go the chandelier lamp that will surely be his next victim if Shiva has not stopped him. "Yes, father?" asked the elephant god at once when walked towards his father who was looking very serious.

"Ganesha, why are you doing all these? have you forgotten. What the *Vedas* say about behaving in one's house?" asked Shiva sternly.

"I have not forgotten the *Vedas*, father. It is just that Kubera is very proud of his wealth as it is my duty to put in a right mind," answered Ganesha solemnly

"I agree, my son," replied Lord Shiva extending his right arm with his palm in supine position. All of a sudden, a roasted rice ball appeared in his palm.

"This is for you, my son. Let this satisfy your hunger," blessed Lord Shiva handling the roasted rice to his son. Ganapathi gulped the rice ball in one go. "I am so full now!" exclaimed Ganapathi rubbing his stomach.

Kubera was astonished when all his food was unable to satisfy the need of Ganesha but single roasted rice could. He looked upon

Lord Shiva puzzled. Lord Shiva understood Kubera's confusion. "It is true that all your food is unable to satisfy Ganesha's hunger. The reason is all your foods is only material and is full of pride. Such things will never satisfy Ganesha's hunger no matter how much you give him." "However, the roasted rice that I gave him is full of devotion and love which is the reason why it satisfies him." explained Shiva looking at Kubera's face.

"Lord, I have learnt my lesson. I promise I would not be so proud of my wealth anymore" said the king of Yakshas humbly.

"It is good that you have learnt your mistake," replied Shiva. "You must remember that too much material richness will cloud one's senses and ability to think, so it is best to keep it in moderate" continued Lord Shiva.

"Ganesha and I must take leave now as it is getting late," said Shiva gripping his trident and with his another hand, he held Ganesha's hand. In a split second both of the gods disappeared from the sight. Kubera had learnt a lesson and he murmured, "Om Namo Shivaya!" Then he carried on with his duties.

NOTE:

Pride is one of the dangerous diseases and it can block the senses and mind. A proud person thinks oneself to be better than the others and so will not accept the opinion of others. Thus, he cannot move forward in life. A proud person is not interested in self realization and as a result he cannot elevate his condition in life. So, always be humble no matter how great you are. Remember -Great persons are always simple person.

THE DELIVERANCE OF THE DEMON VRITRASURA BY INDRA

The demon Vritrasura was once a true bane opposing the gods at the beginning of the creation. The tale of this demon killed by Lord Indra's is narrated here.

Vritrasura; assumed the form of a great serpent. His scales were hard like iron and his fangs appeared to be like mountain summits. This great demon sucked each and every drop of water on Earth. The earth was once a life supporting planet at once become barren and waste. The animals and plants started to die one by one

Unable to see the suffering, the mother Earth knows as Bhumidevi at once started to travel to Lord Brahma's planet known as Brahmaloka. Bhumi assumed shape of a white cow and within few moments, she reached the outskirts of the planet.

Reaching the entrance, she at once walked briskly to Lord Brahma's headquarters. Bhumi entered the golden halls, ignoring the gaze of the other gods walked straight to Lord Brahma who was sitting on his throne. Upon seeing the Lord, Bhumi shifted her shape.

"Let me offer my respect and prayers to Lord Brahma; the creator of the universe," said Bhumi humbly, bowing her head until her golden crown touched the feet of Lord Brahma.

"Let the gods bless you, my child" replied the creator pronating his right hand, blessing Bhumi. "What is the matter, you look aggravated," continued Brahma, narrowing his lotus like eye and tilting his body forward.

"Yes, my lord. I am here to ask assistance since there is a great demon terrorizing Earth," complained Bhumi raising her head and gazing Brahma straight to his eyes.

"Ahh, I see, this demon is a serpent that drained all the drinkable liquids from Earth," answered Brahma quietly.

"How to destroy this demon, my lord," asked one of the gods suddenly interrupting the conversation.

Brahma did not answer the question but he shut his eyes and mumbled something in Sanskrit. After a second, Brahma opened his eyes slowly and he turned to look at Bhumi who was standing like a statue and then glanced over the gods.

"Don't worry Bhumi, the time is ripe for a powerful god to come to existence, He will be the leader of the gods and he will put an end to this demon, don't despair, just be patient," said Brahma in a confident tone.

After hearing the advice of Lord Brahma, Bhumi felt relieved. She thanked Brahma, excused herself and made her way to earth. Time passed on as the earth goddess continues to withstand the suffering and torment of serpent.

Vritra after he made this earthly planet dry went across the skies and confronted the dawn. The dawn personified was known as the Ushas'. They took forms as cows and they were the attendants of the sun god, Surya.

"Ushas', well, well, how are you doing?" mocked Vritra, once he reached the surface of sun where the Ushas' normally are. The Ushas' seemed surprised and they replied trembling, "Vritra, what are you doing here?"

"What am I doing here?" "Well, it is a good question," the serpent answered with his yellow eyes gleaming.

"To capture you, of course!" hissed the serpent again with his terrible forked tongue going in and out.

After hearing the determination of Vritra, the Ushas' attempt to flee, but the demon surrounded the dawn personified with his fat serpentine body. The Ushas' have nowhere to escape. Enclosed within the serpent's body, Vritra then breathed poison from his mouth. The cows fainted one by one. Grinning at the sight of fainted Ushas', Vritrisura tied their legs and put on his back, Vritra reached Earth in no time, carrying the Ushas'.

The Ushas' started to regain consciousness. "Vritra! Let us go, you useless scum!!" Not working. The Ushas' tried to release themselves from the ropes. No use either.

"Help! Help!" they shouted top of their lungs. Vritra breathed deeply ignoring their shouts. He made way to a cave known as Vala.

"Keep quite!" ordered Vritra strictly, once he came to the Vala cave. "You want me to devour all of you, is it?" questioned the demon putting its face near the cows which scared the hearts out of them. The Ushas' shook their heads vigorously. "Good," replied Vritra pulling an evil grin, suddenly pushing the cows into the cave and rolled a boulder to obstruct the entrance. The cows mooed in desperation. Now the dawn personified were imprisoned within the cave.

V. Satish

Aditi; the mother of gods were at the time pregnant with another child when the rampage of Vritra is going on. By the will of Lord Vishnu she gave birth to a golden child in due course of time.

The golden child once born magically stood and exclaimed in a powerful voice, "Where is the demon which is waiting for me to destroy?" The earth rumbled at the child's voice.

Vritra at the moment was at his stone fortress which was known as Dasyu suffered a small trembling too.

"What caused this earthquake?" asked Vritrasura to himself. "Something is terribly wrong in heavens or perhaps the gods had found way to destroy me?"

"Let me wait and see," said Vritra softly to himself. In spite of words of assurance, his heart began to palpitate faster as if death is upon his head.

At the same time, the golden child whom sprang out of Aditi's womb suddenly grew into a young muscular man within seconds. The man wore a golden crown bedecked by jewels. His arms were ripped as if he was working out. He emitted an aura of golden light. Other gods who were present at the heavens began to wonder with astonishment when this child was born.

The air suddenly shimmered as Lord Vishnu with his celebrated symbols appears. All the other gods immediately bowed tipping their head to the Supreme Personality of Godhead. Lord Vishnu blessed them.

Smiling, Sri Vishnu said in a powerful yet gentle voice. "Time has come for Vritra to meet his end, and when it does, water will be released and earth will return to its normal state"

"This man is Indra......" said Lord Vishnu pointing his bluish index finger to the man who stood like a statue, looking attentively to Lord Vishnu.

"He is your king and will be celebrated as the king of heaven," said Sri Vishnu to the assembly of gods. "He is the one who will send Vritra to the superintendent of death and he will lead all of you in never ending war between gods and demons" exclaimed Lord Vishnu and suddenly disappeared.

Indra turned his head to look at the gods who assembled behind him. "So, the demon Vritra had created disturbance, I see," said Indra who is now the king of the gods as well as the heavenly kingdom.

"Hmmm, I will confront this demon now!" said Indra confidently. The king of heaven extended his mighty arm and called upon his mount; which is an albino elephant by the name of Airvata. Decorated with golden plates that covered the tusks and red colour silk garment which was situated on the body, the lord of devas immediately mounted the elephant whom at once trumpeted as if it understood they were riding to war.

"Let go!" shouted Indra. The elephant stormed out of hall and like a rocket, pummelled downwards with an unimaginable speed for an elephant. Within seconds, Airvata penetrated the Earth's atmosphere and eventually stepped on a barren wasteland. The effect of Airvata's landing had created a small tremor that radiated in four directions.

Indra surveyed the wasteland with his golden eyes. The wasteland is just a desert with red colour sand extending as far as the eye could see. He got down from his elephant, and narrowed his eyes. After some moment of surveying the desert; his eyes caught a fortress which was made out of granite stones.

Grinning to himself, the lord of devas mounted on his elephant. He yoked the beast and it rose to the air and shot the fortress. Airvata stopped at the entrance of the great fortress. Indra got down his mount, patted its trunk and walked into the fort unarmed.

The stone fortress is actually the dwelling of Vritrasura who was at the time sipping wine at his throne. Just beside him, there is a very large sphere which holds upon all the deities of water. They hammer the sphere with their bare hands, but were flung to the other end of the sphere.

Vritrasura suddenly heard a loud sound coming from a room beside the main hall. The demon put down the glass, smacked its lips using its horrible forked tongue. The demon then walked to the source of noise, stopping for a moment and showed his tongue to the captured deities in the sphere mocking them and then continued its journey.

Indra who was wrestling with the guards looked at the hallway when he heard great thumping sound which rattled the ground.

Indra narrowed his eyes and soon a giant serpent with legs made ways towards him. Indra punched the guard strongly and knocked him flat. Blood flowed from the guard's chin and he passed out. Indra steadied himself as Vritra began to advance towards him angrily.

The demon opened its mouth which resembled like a big mountain cave. Indra at once stopped the demon and said, "Let's fight outside."

"If you wanted, let's go," accepted the demon. In an eye blink, they flew upwards towards the roof of the palace, breaking it and reached the clouds.

"Now, you will meet your end!" exclaimed Indra in a confident voice. "Lets see about it," answered Vritra and at once charged at Indra. However Indra caught hold of the demon's teeth which was just like small mountains and the serpent could not move.

Indra whirled the snake and threw him using his newly found godly strength. The demon flew and dropped from the air to the ground with a loud thud. Indra descended smoothly and landed on the ground not far from the mildly passed out serpent.

After a while, Vritra began to gain consciousness. Shaking its reptile head to drive away the dizziness, it set its gleaming yellow eyes on Indra. The demon, again with great anger and strength rushed towardsthe god with its mouth open.

As soon as Vritra reached him, Indra at once strangled the serpent using his mighty arm. Vritra's throat at once choked and the demon spluttered. As drops of perspiration began to fall, the demon threw its legs hither tighter. One of its giant reptilian leg caught Indra and this caused Indra to fly backwards and rolled before coming to complete halt. "My strength is going away!!" he screamed within his heart. Blood dripped from his face. One kick from the demon, his strength began to fade. Surely another kick would kill him.

Realising that his foe is too strong for now, Indra vanished from the sight and appeared beside his elephant. Vritra suddenly saw Indra vanished and traced him to Airvata, the demon grinned its snaky grin. Without wasting a moment, Indra climbed and yoked his elephant which vanished. "Bahh, what a coward!" exclaimed Vritra to himself before entering his fortress.

Indra came to the heavens and entered the throne room with a gloomy and bloody face. He saw his brothers (other gods) waiting enthusiastically for him.

"What happened?" asked Vayudeva,

"Is Vritra dead?" asked Agni excitedly.

"No, the demon is too strong," answered Indra and he crashed on a seat. "I think I need weapon to kill the serpent but the weapon must suit me" said Indra slowly to the assembly of gods who were standing around him.

"Then, there is only one path," said Varuna solemnly.

"What is it?" asked Indra excitedly.

"You need to meditate to Lord Vishnu." replied the god of water and sea. "Why is that?" asked Indra. "Nothing escapes from the Supreme Personality of Godhead, everything comes from Him and He is everything."

"He surely will give you a solution regarding the weapon" said Vayu

"There is nothing He doesn't know," Agni quickly answered

"That is true, all of us, gods including you, Lord Brahma and even Lord Shiva are below Lord Vishnu's jurisdiction," added Vayudeva solemnly.

"Then, I think I need to meditate unto him," answered Indra rising from the seat.

"That is what I said", mumbled Varuna.

Indra disappeared and appeared at a mountain. Without wasting time, Indra climbed the mountain and reached the peak.

He flexed his mighty arms, withdrew a deep breath and started to meditate upon the Supreme Lord. After many years, Lord Vishnu who was lying on the causal ocean opened his eyes waking up from his *yoga nidram* position. Then, He vanished from His abode and appeared in front of Indra who was still closing his eyes and murmuring the words, 'Narayana'.

Due to the blinding effulgence that emanates from Lord Vishnu's body, Indra opened eyes. The king of heaven saw the Supreme Lord decorated with his four celebrated symbols-namely the mace, conch shell, disc and a lotus flower smiling. Indra got up to his knees and prostrated in front of Sri Vishnu.

"My dear Lord, You are the Supreme Personality of Godhead. You are the Supreme soul and possess supreme knowledge" "Please, my Lord, provide me with a solution to kill Vritra."

"My dear king of heavens, to deliver the serpentine demon, you need to seek out a sage. His name is Dadichi. He has been meditating for a very long time. The time has come for him to return to Me. You must take his spine and it will kill Vritra" answered Vishnu and immediately disappeared.

Indra quickly climbed down the mountain. "Vayudeva!" yelled Indra as he reached the base. The air shimmered when the lord of wind appeared in front of him.

"Listen here Vayu, there is no time to explain. I need to know where is the dwelling place of sage Dadichi?" asked Indra anxiously.

"Not far from here, head towards the eastern side and soon you will see a hut that is belongs to Dadichi" replied Vayu, "Where are you ....?" began Vayu but Indra already stormed towards the eastern direction. Sighing, Vayu disappeared.

Indra in no time reached his destination. He saw the sage clad in orange cloth, and with his possessions, namely the hammer and a water pot beside him. The sage closed his eyes and was in midst of meditation. Indra felt an aura of power radiating from the body of the sage.

The king of heaven walked slowly to the sage and bowed. "My dear sage Dadichi, I am Indra, the king of heavens" introduced Indra. Dadichi opened his eyes slowly and replied "I have waited long time for you, Devendra. The world's situation is dire. Vritra has gone too much. It is time that you should end the serpent's terror and released the Ushas."

"I know that but I require your help." said Indra slowly rubbing his hands.

"Hmm, I see, you need my spine don't you, my dear Devendra?" answered Dadichi smiling.

"Uh ...oh ...yes," replied Indra. The old sage said' "My time in this mortal world is over, I am going to achieve *Moksha*" "After I leave my body, you can take my spine and use it to kill the demon."

Dadichi closed his eyes and suddenly a bright light exited from the top of the sage's head and flew up to the space. The moment the light flew, the sage's body suddenly crumpled like sand. However, only his backbone remained.

Reaching out his trembling hands, Indra gripped the spine which resembled an iron rod. Gulping, he looked upon the sky and said, "My dear sage Dadichi, you have sacrificed yourself for me to obtain your spine, I promise you that I will kill this demon"

Without any moment to lose, Indra returned to his heavenly abode holding Dadichi's spine. As he entered the hall, other gods greeted him and enquired where he had gone.

"There is no time to explain," answered Indra quickly. "Who can properly fashion this spine?" asked Indra glancing at the gods. "Well I can try," said one of the gods known as Visvakarma. Visvakarma is the engineer of the gods. "Then, quickly do it," said Indra handing the spine to Visvakarma.

Visvakarma received the spine carefully as if it was made out of glass. He summoned his tools like the hammer and other mechanics. Magically, the tools began hammering and shaping Dadichi's spine accompanied by loud noises. All the other gods stood around Visvakarma who was controlling his tools by flicking his hands rhythmically.

In few moments, the tools stopped working by themselves. The spine now looks like two spheres at both ends and the middle is a handle made from pure gold. It flew to Indra who caught it. As Indra held the weapon, the spheres at both ends emitted electrical waves. Indra opened his palm and the weapon flew into it. "I will call this *Vajrayudha*", murmured Indra inspecting his new weapon. He closed his fist as the thunderbolt begins to emit electrical sparks. The king of heaven smiled and as he gripped it stronger.

"Vritra, your demise is here!" he yelled suddenly. The other gods looked in awe as Indra flew towards Airvata and screamed with power, "Airvata lets us go and finish this serpent once and for all!"

The elephant trumpeted. It understood its master's determination and in a great speed travelled to Vritra's fortress.

"Come out, you useless demon, lets fight!" yelled Indra, his eyes full of anger and his body surged with waves of energy. Suddenly Indra heard loud noise that rattle the ground when the serpent came out from its fortress.

Its yellow reptilian eyes gleamed as it saw Indra on the albino elephant floating on the sky. Vritrasura propelled itself and rose to meet Indra. "Well, well, you are a coward, Indra, since before this you fled" shouted Vritra.

"It is because I have no weapon at that time, you dumb!" answered Indra.

"Hmm! Have you now?!" asked Vritra sarcastically.

Indra did not reply but raised his new weapon which generated electric pulses.

Vritra narrowed its eyes for the serpent has never seen the weapon before. "Bah! Whatever is it but no weapon can kill me!" said Vritra showing its forked tongue.

"Don't brag so much Vritra as your fate is sealed now and you will enter hell,". Vritra hissed. "You are the first to taste my thunderbolt," screamed Indra. With full strength, he hurled the *Vajra* to the serpent.

Vritra opened its mouth to swallow it but unfortunatey the *vajra* flew above the demon's body, made a U-turn and striked the body. "Ahhh!!" yelled Vritra with agonizing pain.

Vajra flew back to Indra like a boomerang and Indra caught it. The king of devas closed his eyes and murmured, "Lord Vishnu, please makes me successful." He opened his eyes just in time to see Vritra rushing towards him exhibiting its poisonous fangs.

Startled, Indra threw this thunderbolt again and this time it struck Vritra with a loud sound. The whole sky lit with bright light and lighting flashed through the sky.

"Ahhhh!!" cried Vritra loudly and as the great serpent died screaming, there was tremendous vibration on the earth and in the sky, in all directions.

The serpent fell straight from the sky to the ground with enourmous noise. Vritra opened its fierce mouth and its teeth were just like mountain summits. Its body extended for more than ten miles. Thus, the life of this demon has expired and it passed to kingdom of Yama.

Indra clasped his thunderbolt. He let out a whistle which was relief. He descended from Airvata and made way to Vritra's fortress. Entering the demon's abode, Indra walked quickly to the main hall.

He saw a sphere holding the aquatic deities. Indra broke the sphere with his fist which is powerful like mountains. Once released the deities burst out, turned and bowed to Indra. "Thank you, lord" Wihin seconds, earth gets flooded. Indra walked out from the stone fortress, and using his *vajrayudha*, he smashed the fortress. It crumpled like dust and washed away by waters

After releasing the captured waters, Indra made his way to the cave where Ushas' were imprisoned. He rolled the boulder and released the cows.

"My dear Indra, thank you for releasing us" said the Ushas' in unison. "Welcome, it is my duty," answered Indra, smilling. The Ushas' circumbulated Indra and shot up to the sky to meet their master, the sun god.

The king of devas saw that the sky is very near to the earth. Empowering himself, Indra used his mighty arms and pushes up the sky.

The gods who watched from the sky get overwhelmed with joy and they showered flowers on Indra who returned to the heavenly kingdom with victory killing Vritrasura, releasing the water, releasing the dawn personified and even pushing up the sky.

NOTE:

The *Rig Veda* has dedicated around three fourth of total hymns to Indra. The *Rig Veda* often refers him as Sakra (mighty one). This tale tells his heroic defeat of Vritra, liberating the waters, smashing the cave enclosure known as Vala where Ushas' were imprisoned in my own way

Indra is the god of war. He also controls all the villages, cattle, chariots, waters and horses.

One verse in *Rig Veda* reads:

He under whose supreme control are horses, all chariots, the villages and cattle.

He who gave beings to the Sun and Morning, who leads the waters. He O man is Indra (2.12.7-*Rig Veda*; translation Griffith).

THE TALE OF LORD BALARAMA'S MARRIAGE TO REVATHI

Lord Balarama was the elder brother of Lord Krishna. He is said to be the incarnation of Lord Sesa. (multihooded serpent Lord Vishnu resides). Ananta Sesa is the serpent that not only where Lord Vishnu resides but it holds different planet in their position.

Lord Balarama accompanies Lord Krishna when He descends to establish the principles of religion. In other words, Lord Balarama is none other than Sri Krishna because Bhaktivedanta Swami explained that Balarama is an immediate expansion of Krishna. Here is an interesting tale involving His marriage to Revathi.

Once upon a time, there lived a person called as King Kakudmi. In Mahabharata, it is said that Kakudmi is also called as Ravaita (Son of Revata).

King Kakudmi ruled over a kingdom of Kusasthali, which was a prosperous and advanced kingdom under the sea. Although King Ravaita is a mortal, he was endowed with some mystic powers. He can travel across space and even to the highest material planet called as Brahmaloka to seek an audience with Lord Brahma. To travel and seek audience with Brahma is not possible for even the great mystic yogis couldn't go, but this Kusasthali king has obtained such privilege.

King Kakudmi has a daughter by the name of Revathi. Princess Revathi was very beautiful. Her eyes are just like lotus flower and her lips are rosy, while her teeth glittered like shinning pearls. In short, Revathi has all the auspicious qualifications for a lady.

One day, King Kakudmi called upon Revathi from her quarters. Revathi immediately put upon her jewels and replied to her maid servant who was standing beside her, "I want you to go to my father and announce that I am coming in a while."

"Yes, lady," said the maid bowing and walked out from the quarters. The maid made her way to the throne room. "King, princess Revathi said that she is coming", said the maid respectfully kneeling in front of the great king.

The king grunted and at that moment Princess Revathi entered the throne room. She looked dazzling with her thin waist and raised breasts. When she entered, she stole the attention of her father's ministers and secretaries who was present at that moment.

Looking upon his ministers' attention to his daughter, the king purposely made a grunting sound in his throat. Hearing this sound, the ministers tried to act in front of the king by inspecting some papers. Revathi bowed in front of her father.

"My dear Revathi, the time is ripe for you to marry and enter into householder life." said Kakudmi loudly as if asking her to enter the householder life there and then.

"Do you have anyone in mind?" asked Kakudmi rising from his throne and walked towards his daughter.

"I have no one in my mind, my dear father," answered Revathi slowly.

"Then we have a big problem here," replied Kakudmi. Revathi slowly gazed at her father's wrinkled face.

"I could not understand father. What sort of problem are you talking about?" asked Revathi confused.

"I have no one in my mind either", said Kakudmi standing in front of Revathi.

"But I have prepared a list of candidates…" continued the king pulling out a roll of paper from his shirt. He handed it to Revathi and said in a gentle fatherly voice, "I want you to see the candidates and make up your mind".

Revathi did not receive the paper but replied, "My dear father, if you couldn't make up your mind, then how you would expect me to make up my mind?" asked Revathi. "Hmmm, if that is the case, I think we need to seek advice from Lord Brahma regarding your future bride", suggested Kakudmi.

"Yes, I agree with you, father." replied Revathi. Without wasting any moment, both of them travelled through the space and ultimately reached Lord Brahma's planet known as Brahmaloka.

Upon reaching Brahmaloka, King Kakudmi and Princess Revathi saw that numerous beings present there. Lord Brahma and his wife, Goddesses Saraswathi was seated at their golden throne and enjoying dance performances by the celestial dancers known as the Gandharvas.

King Kakudmi beckoned Revathi to remain silent and they waited patiently until the performances were over. After a while, the performances concluded and the dancers started to dismiss. Seeing that their chance is here, King Kakudmi quickly made his way towards Lord Brahma, followed eagerly by Revathi.

"I offer my respectful obeisance to you, Lord Brahma; the creator of this universe. I am here to ask for an advice."

"Nice to see you King Kakudmi. What advice do you seek?"

"Lord Brahma, this is my daughter Revathi," said King Kakudmi and at the same time beckoned his beautiful daughter forward. As Revathi came forward, she offered her respectful obeisance and prayers to Lord Brahma.

"I cannot find a suitable match for her and this is the reason why I have come here so that you can offer me advice."

Lord Brahma replied, "Hmmm, I see, do you have anyone in mind, my dear good king."

"Actually, I have prepared a list of candidates that I feel that they are of suitable match for my daughter but I could not make my mind."

"Let me see the list."

"Here is it," said Kakudmi, handing over a paper to the god who was sitting on his golden throne. The paper floated and made its way towards Brahma. The creator caught the floating paper and opened it. His pupils moved left and right as he inspected the names. Suddenly, he smiled as if the paper is a joke and unable to suppress his emotions, he laughed loudly.

Kakudmi and Revathi looked at each other, astonished at Lord Brahma's behaviour. Humbly, the king asked, "My Lord, what is the matter?"

Lord Brahma finished his laughter and answered, "My dear king, the candidates that you presented me have already passed away, so do their sons, grandsons and descendants."

"But... how is that even possible?" King Kakudmi stammered, astonished. Revathi felt like wanted to pass out in shock.

"My dear King of Kusasthali kingdom, you must know that time flows differently in different planets of existence. The short time that you and your daughter waited to see me causes billions of years passed on Earth."

"Then, who will marry my daughter?", asked the king very surprised at this information. Apparently, he has no knowledge about the supreme time.

This incident of King Kakudmi spent few minutes on Brahmaloka but actually caused billions of years to pass on earth is an example of time travel. Scientists of this modern age tried to create some machine that can bring us back or forward in time but are not successful. However even before the existence of human technology, time travel had been possible.

"Do not despair Kakudmi, now it is Dvapara Yuga on earth and Lord Vishnu took incarnation as Lord Krishna and Lord Balarama," "Try to ask for their hand", suggested Brahma with twinkling in his eyes.

"Yes, I certainly will." "Thank you, Lord," replied King Kakudmi. Lord Brahma raised his right palm which was decorated with the sacred symbol Om, and blessed them.

Father and daughter made way out of the highest material planet hurriedly and headed to earth.

They reached their destination in no time. However what they saw shocked their brains. It is no more the planet earth that they knew. Revathi gaped open her mouth while her father closed his eyes for a second for the scene is a total eye sore for him.

Kakudmi opened his eyes slowly and immediately everything seemed small. Trees, people, buildings and everything seemed tiny. Both of them saw that people dwindled in stature. In other words, they saw that humans have shrunken ultimately and both of them looked like giants.

The people shuffled past them. They looked exactly like dolls, tiny and their movements were fast like ants, scrambling here and there. Revathi and Kakudmi looked upon each other in surprise.

"Giants! Demons!" Kakudmi heard a scream. He turned his head and so does Revathi. One old man with a walking stick, stood frozen holding to his walking stick and pointing at the king with his trembling hands.

"We are not giants, fool! We need to find Lord Balarama. Where will he be?" said Revathi angrily advancing towards the man. He immediately yelled and crouched. "Lord Balarama is in the city of Dvaraka, twenty miles from here." replied the feeble man pointing towards the eastern direction.

"Thanks! Come on", gestured Kakudmi to her daughter. Kakudmi and Revathi flew to the east. People there was taken aback seeing them in the air. "What are they?" asked one woman to her friend. "Demons I think, don't worry Krishna will end their lives in a second", her friend replied confidently still looking at the sky where Kakudmi and Revathi went leaving behind trail of smoke.

They sped to the eastern direction and in no time reached the city which was well fortified within the sea.

The people at Dvaraka that two beings as big as building flying in the sky. Kakudmi and Revathi landed at the courtyard smoothly causing people of Dvaraka screaming and running helter skelter.

Lord Balarama at that time was praying to Lord Shiva when He heard the citizens screaming. Feeling slightly agitated, the lord stopped his prayers and came out of the temple to see the commotion

He stopped a woman who was running like being chased by a ghost. "Why are you running? What happened?" asked Balarama

"My dear Balarama, there are two beings at the size of buildings walking towards the main city", replied the woman occasionally turning her head afraid as if Kakudmi and Revathi may appear there and then.

"Dont be afraid," said Lord Balarama looking at the sky. "I will see this beings", He continued. Balarama called upon his weapon which is a plow which suddenly appeared in his hand. He grasped it and marched leaving the woman gaping.

He came to the courtyard and saw Kakudmi and Revathi standing and turning their head left and right as if finding someone.

"Who are you people and what is your purpose of coming to Dvaraka, scaring the citizens?", questioned Balarama loudly. Kakudmi blinked when he heard the powerful voice. Immediately, he knew that they had found Lord Balarama as the lord who appeared before them must be the Supreme Personality of Godhead who emitted light from His body.

Kakudmi and Revathi simultaneously dropped down just like a stick to the feet of the Lord. Bhaktivedanta Swami stated that the act of offering respect to a senior Vaishnava is to fall down exactly like a stick. Lord Balarama was astonished and in reflex action He asked them to rise. "Who are you people, actually?" questioned the Lord resting His muscular hand on His plow.

"My dear Lord Balarama, I am King Kakudmi of the Kusasthala kingdom and this is my daughter by the name of Revathi" "Lord of Universe, please take my daughter as your wife", said Kakudmi humbly.

Lord Balarama looked upon Revathi. She was so much taller than Him. Lord Balarama jumped and using His plow, He tapped gently on Revathi's head. Thus, Revathi shrunk to normal height of humans of that age. Lord Balarama put His arm around Revathi's waist and said, "Kakudmi, I accept your daughter, let the marriage be celebrated today!"

The marriage between the Supreme Personality of Godhead and the daughter of King Kakudmi was duly celebrated with great pomp and splendour. After marriage, Kakudmi said to Lord Balarama, "My dear Lord, you hold the planets with Your million heads. You are the original Supreme Personality of Godhead, please excuse me as my fatherly duties are over. I must go to Badrikashama and meditate upon Lord Vishnu"

"Kakudmi, I permit you to go to Badrikashama. May your meditation to the supreme Lord be successful", replied Lord Balarama. Upon taking the permission and bidding goodbye to his daughter, king Kakudmi went off on his way to northern direction to engage in austerities and penances.

NOTE:

Time factor as being discussed in this tale of Kakudmi journey to Brahmaloka and finding billions of years have passed on earth is a sign that no being is more powerful than time. Time is most powerful because it is the representation of Lord Vishnu. No beings can manipulate time. Materialistic people may try to trample the forces of time by creating time- machine but it will not work out. Remember, due to time factor this universe is created and destroyed.

THE TALE OF GREAT SAGE BHRIGU AND THE GODS OF HINDU TRINITY

Once upon a time, the sage and ascetic among the gods, Narada patrolled the universe. He was strumming his *veena* and chanting the verse, 'Narayana' as usual. Suddenly, he stopped, floating in the space and peered downwards. Unknowingly, he had already reached earth.

"I have not visited earth for a long time, only God knows the condition of these inhabitants." "I shall go now," said the great sage Narada and he descended smoothly and landed on the bank of a river called as Sarasvathi. Narada walked briefly along the river. He suddenly stopped when he saw some thick, smoke rising to the sky.

"Hmm, some sages are performing sacrifices", mumbled Narada. "I haven't caused any quarrels for some time, and I think now is the best time," thought Narada gleefully.

Thinking so, he walked further downstream along the river and ultimately, he found a group of sages were sitting around the fire and busily chanting *mantras*. Feeling very anxious to stir trouble, the great sage Narada said loudly, "Hail sages!"

Upon hearing the voice of Narada, the sages stood up and bowed respectfully. Smiling, Narada blessed them asking all of them to take their seat. "What is the purpose of this sacrifice?" inquired Narada. One of the sages stood up and answered, "My dear Narada, we are doing this sacrifice for the benefit of mankind."

"Hmm......" Narada shook his head slowly. The sages looked each other in surprise due to Narada's action that seemed like disagreeing with the events of the sacrifice. One sage asked humbly, "Why are you shaking your head?

The great sage Narada answered in a very thoughtful tone, "As you all know, all the effect of sacrifice are done to please a particular god. So, can I know which trinity of gods do you all wish the sacrifice will be directed to?"

The group of sages were dumbfounded for a moment. Obviously, it didn't struck their mind that which god should they direct the sacrifice.

"I think Lord Shiva is the suitable god," suggested one slim sage. "Why do you say so?" asked another sage in very commanding tone.

"Lord Shiva is the master of this world, he is the one who is responsible for every affairs of this world, so I think that the sacrifice were go to him, because all of us, humans are subjected to his decision" answered the slim sage confidently.

"I don't think so, I think Lord Vishnu is the most suitable person because, He is the Supreme Personality of Godhead and is the king of the gods, even Lord Shiva is under him" said another.

"Are you trying to say that Lord Shiva is not the suitable god?" asked the slim sage angrily.

"Yes, because it is the truth!" answered the sage who suggested Lord Vishnu. The slim sage eyes turned red and he prepared to fight with the slim sage, when a plumped sage raised his hand and said, "Stop!" "Neither Vishnu nor Shiva is suitable enough to gain the benefit of this sacrifice, but I think Lord Brahma is the most suitable person."

Upon hearing the words of the plump sage, the other two sages turned to him and pounced on him exactly like a tiger pounces on a deer. The plump sage fall with a thud and big commotion happen there.

Looking at the fight, Narada thought, "Finally, the commotion is initiated, but I shall cause further complication."

He shouted top of his voice, "Stop!"

The sages stopped fighting and stood up, covered with dirt and mud.

"You are sages, not animals! There is no need to quarrel over the most suitable god to receive the offer of the sacrifice.", Narada said angrily.

"Then how are we going to decide the suitable god?" asked the plump sage breathing heavily.

"Listen, one of you must test each god of the Trinity and which god passes the test shall be the one who will receive the effect of sacrifice" Narada suggested.

"Then let me go and test them!," offered the slim sage, walking forward. "No, you haven't gain sufficient knowledge to test them," said Narada holding up his hand. The sage stopped walking at once.

"Then, who can test them?" he asked curiously. "I think the sage Bhrigu is the most suitable candidate to carry out this dangerous task." suggested Narada. "Right!, Good choice, Narada!", replied the thin sage.

The great sage, Bhrigu stepped forward confidently. All the other sage bowed to him as he is a great sage living from the beginning of time and one of the Manas Putras. "I shall carry out the test," he said in a grave voice.

Narada smiled and replied, "So be it, Bhrigu I hope you will be successful." Bhrigu bowed in front of Narada and in a blink of an eye, he disappeared from the sight with a clap of thunder. Narada blessed the sages and went on his way.

Without any moment to lose, Bhrigu travelled in the space and made way to his father's planet.

He stopped in the middle of universe, just below Brahmaloka and descended. He penetrated the atmosphere and reached Lord Brahma's palace in no time.

Bhrigu saw that many beings were present in the hall of Lord Brahma's palace and they were listening to Brahma's speech regarding the do's and don'ts of lives. Suddenly, Bhrigu stormed into hall and without paying respect to his father, the sage sat on an empty seat arrogantly. All those who are present were astonished at Bhrigu's improper action. They turned to look at Lord Brahma who seemed very angry. Brahma cannot tolerate his son's action and he got agitated immediately.

Lord Brahma said in loudly, "Bhrigu you have learnt all the *vedas* and you should know how to respect your parents!" "You are very impolite, so be prepared to receive my curse!"

Goddess Sarasvathi who was sitting beside Lord Brahma at once provoked Lord Brahma's quality of goodness and asked him not to be angry. After listening to Sarasvathi pleas, Lord Brahma controlled his anger with great intelligence.

Bhrigu saw how Brahma got agitated with a minor disrespect, and thus the sage concluded that Brahma is certainly not fit to receive the effect of the sacrifice. Thinking so, Bhrigu disappeared from the hall without saying anything and appeared in Kailash; the residency of Lord Shiva.

Bhrigu appeared at the entrance of the private apartment of Lord Shiva. He closed his eyes for a moment to experience the soothing coldness and then he opened his eyes slowly.

The sage made a beeline towards the private entranced which was guarded by two guards. When Bhrigu reached the guards, one of the guards said in a loud voice, "Please stop, you cannot enter inside!" "Why is it so?" Bhrigu asked slightly agitated. "Lord Shiva and Parvathi Devi are having their private time, no one is allowed to enter!" the guard answered in commanding tone.

Bhrigu flew into rage. He has not been denied to enter before in any circumstances. The great sage flicked his hand and the guard flew and slammed against the metal door and fall into state of unconsciousness.

Bhrigu walked past the guard and pushed the tightly shut metal door with his immense yogic power. Then, he walked slowly into the room searching for Lord Shiva with his fearful eyes which was like a lion preying on a deer.

His eyes caught the sight of Lord Shiva and his wife, Parvathi was dancing. Lord Shiva when entered dancing motion, was celebrated with the name of Nadaraja. Nadaraja means 'Lord of the Dances.' The dance itself is called as Bharatanatyam and the dance performed by Parvathi is called as Lasa.

During their dancing motion, Parvathi's sari was drenched with sweat and causes her breasts and thighs to be exposed to the sage. Parvathi upon realizing the appearance of Bhrigumuni grew ashamed and as an act of reflex moved to the corner of the room with her face hung downwards in utter shame. Shiva realised the entrance of Bhrigu to the private chamber and the subsequent retraction of Parvathi to the corner of the room without any prior notice.

Shiva flew into rage and he rushed to Bhrigu who was still standing there arrogantly. Lord Shiva shouted at the top of his voice, "Bhrigumuni, people and even gods fear you as you learnt the *vedas* and acquire supreme knowledge regarding the universe!"

"But, it is shameful that you although very great as you seem, forget your manners that you must not enter a room without permission!" continued Mahadeva, pointing his left index finger to Parvathi who is still standing at the corner with her head hung down.

Shiva took his greatest weapon, *Trisula*; a three pointed trident and subsequently aimed at Bhrigu's neck. The lord said in a very commanding tone, "Since, you have no respect and manners, I shall teach you a lesson that you will not forget!"

The lord of destruction lunged forward the trident, but however Bhrigu was not at all afraid. He knew no beings can stop the trident and he braced himself to death. So, he just stood there like a marble statue without wanting to run away hide. However Parvathi came forward.

Parvathi said in soothing voice, "My dear husband, you are the lord of the three worlds, please forgive Bhrigu as he is your son and is still small. He had unknowingly made a mistake."

Hearing His consort's soothing words, the three eyed god sighed and simultaneously lowered his trident. "It is better you get out from here, Bhrigu!" thundered Lord Shiva.

Bhrigu made his way out of the palace as quickly as his legs could carry him. When he is outside Kailash, Bhrigu exhaled deeply and decided that not even Mahadeva is fit enough to receive the effect of the sacrifice.

Without any moment to spare, the son of Lord Brahma vanished and appeared at the atmosphere. He walked in a fast pace to his next destination, Vaikuntha planet in order to meet Sri Vishnu.

Bhrigumuni crossed this material universe which was described as dark. Within seconds, he came to a place where there is only light. The light is what is known as *Brahmajyoti* or the effulgence of Brahman itself.

According to Bhaktivedanta Swami, the *brahmajyoti* is the destination of the impersonalists known as the Vedantists. The Vedantists are those people who studied the *Vedas* and are masters in that aspect. But these kinds of people fail to realise the goal of *Vedas*. In other words, the *Vedas* are indirect way to a destination. The ultimate goal of *Vedas* is Lord Vishnu or His incarnations. By reading the *Vedas*, one will come to the Supreme Lord's existence (liberation) eventually but clearly it is not easy and will take very, very, very long time. This is explained by Lord Krishna in the *Bhagavad-Gita*; 'After many, many births, a wise philosopher surrenders unto Me'. The very word 'wise philosopher' means the impersonalists or the Vedantists. The lord is telling the world that eventually those who conduct the difficult Vedic ritualistic ceremony and observing many restrictions and worshipping each and every god stated in the *Vedas*, they will achieve liberation (*Mukthi*).

In the book KRSNA, it is very clearly explained that there are the classes of men who take into account that the impersonal Brahman effulgence is the origin cause of everything. However, it is not accepted by Vaishnavas as the whole creation rests on Brahman effulgence (*Brahmajyoti*) but the Brahman effulgence itself rests on Vishnu. This is the ultimate fact.

After passing through this spiritual light, the son of Lord Brahma came to vision with the planet Vaikuntha. Bhrigu entered the vast spiritual water known as Karana Ocean. Upon the sage's entrance, the waters of Karana Ocean became greatly agitated and strong wind began blowing upon Bhrigu's entrance to the Ocean of Reason. Bhrigu felt frightened at this sudden change of weather, and quickly he dived into the waters of Karana making way to the ocean bed.

At the ocean bed, there is a great palace with thousand of pillars and with glittering jewels. Bhrigumuni made his way quickly to the main hall where Lord Vishnu is. Reaching the hall, Bhrigu saw the Supreme Personality of Godhead was lying on his snake bed known as Ananta Sesa. He looks like He has been sleeping and his chest which was strong like mountain rose and fall as He breaths.

The son of Brahma suddenly rushed to the Lord and strongly kicked him on the chest. Lord Vishnu opened his lotus like eyes and saw Bhrigu standing. "My dear child, what is you purpose of coming here from earth?" the lord asked gently waking up and gesturing the sage to sit beside him.

Bhrigu felt bewildered for a moment. 'Is my mind playing tricks upon me?". Bhrigu asked himself. Understanding Bhrigu's confusion, Lord Vishnu smiled and taking up the sage feet, said in a soothing voice, "My dear Bhrigu, I am very sorry that your soft, lotus like feet is painful as my chest is a strong as a thunderbolt"

Saying so, Lord Vishnu massaged the sage's feet. In doing so, Lord pressed the 'third eye' which came bulging at the sole of the feet. It is said that when a person falls in a category of false pride, an eye will appear at the sole of the feet. This eye is of course is invisible to mortal eyes but not to God like Lord Vishnu.

The massaging of Lord Vishnu causes the 'third eye' to disappear. Immediately Bhrigu's pride and confusion left him. The sage said, "My Lord, although I kicked your chest you have not slightly agitated, but you are massaging my feet. I must truly admit that I could not understand your actions."

"Bhrigumuni; I know that you have not purposely kicked my chest. You did this to see which of us *Trimurti* is most suitable in receiving the effect of the sacrifice" "It is not a great offense," pacified Lord Vishnu.

Bhrigu stood and said, "My dear Lord Vishnu, it is true that I have tested the *Trimurtis* to see which god is most suitable to receive the effect of the sacrifice and it is You. You are the greatest of all and you alone are fit to obtain the effect."

Lord Vishnu smiled and replied in a gentle voice, "Of course Bhrigu. I will be there at the end of the sacrifice to receive the effect." Bhrigu bowed and took leave from Vaikunta. He travelled across the universe and in no time reached the earthly planet.

Very eager to share his experience, Bhrigu hurriedly made way to the bank of Sarasvathi River.

Reaching the banks, the sage Bhrigu narrated the incident and the assembly of sages concluded that Lord Vishnu is the greatest of the Trinity and is most suitable personality to receive the effects of the sacrifice.

NOTE:

This tale shows that great personalities are always forgiving. Bhaktivedanta Swami explained about this very beautifully and clearly in his book; KRSNA. He gave the example of a small lamp will get agitated by little breeze, but the greatest lamp; the Sun is never disturbed even by the greatest hurricane. Thus, one's greatness is to be measured by one's ability to withstand provoking situation.

THE TALE OF KALANTAKA SHIVA - THE ENDER OF DEATH

Once upon a time, there lived a sage by the name of Mrikandu. He was a great devotee of Lord Shiva and lived at the south Vilvavanam, which is the modern day of Thirukkadavor. Mrikandu and his wife; Marudhamati are devoid of any child since they were married.

Time passes on and soon Mrikandu couldn't take the situation any longer. He decided it is time for him to turn to Lord Shiva.

"My dear Lord of the universe, many years I have been married, but my wife could not conceive a child all this years. Please my lord, by your grace, bless me with a child", prayed Mrikandu every single day.

The sage started to undergo penance vigorously when he will not eat anything and just survive with his breath. Lord Shiva immediately pleased by the meditation measures taken by Mrikandu.

This is the supreme meditation. The core of any meditation is first to control the rhythms of breathing. All the air holes must be blocked and the mind must focus on the god's image, depending on who is the god.

After few years, Lord Shiva was pleased with severe austerities taken by Mrikandu. Thus, Shiva with his trident appeared in front of Mrikandu, who was still engrossed with the meditation. "My dear Mrikandu, your penance is successful, for here I am." Nilakhanta said

Mrikandu opened his eyes and he saw Lord Shiva standing before him. Immediately, he bowed and touched lotus feet of Lord Shiva. Lord Shiva grew compassionate towards his devotee and he raised Mrikandu with his strong arms.

Lord Shiva smiled and said, "You can ask any boon you like."

Mrikandu, still folding his hands, replied, "Lord Shiva, please grant me and my wife a son."

Upon hearing the request of Mrikandu, Lord Shiva asked, "Mrikandu, is it you want me to bless virtuous son who would live for only 16 years or is it you want 100 foolish sons who would live for a long period of time?"

Mrikandu thought about the Lord's offer and finally said, "Please bless me with one virtuous son who will live for only 16 years."

"So, be it" said Lord Shiva and disappeared.

As blessed by the three-eyed lord, Mrikandu's wife gave birth to a son. The couple named their son as Markendeya. As time passes by, Markendeya grew into vitreous boy. Just like his father, Markendeya was very devoted to Lord Shiva. Besides Lord Shiva, he is also devoted to other gods. Being extremely clever, he learnt about many of the gods secrets.

Time and tide waits for no man and the time for Markendeya to give up his life is near. Markendeya tried to fight the fate entrusted to him, that he will die in his 16th year. He thought and finally made a decision to meditate upon Lord Brahma since Lord Brahma is the wisest in this particular universe.

After meditating for almost a year, Brahma appeared in front of Markendeya. He asked, "Markendeya, what is the purpose you called me?"

"My dear Lord Brahma, as fate foretold, I would give up my life in my 16th year. Please, tell me any solution to escape death as I don't want to die so early. I wanted to preach more about Lord Shiva to mankind." replied Markendeya.

Hearing Markendeya's statement, Brahma said gently, "Your fate is tied to Shiva as he is the reason why you are born. However, I shall teach you the mantra of death repellent. If you utter this mantra, the Lord of Death; Yamaraja cannot come near you"

And so Brahma taught Markendeya the Mahamrityunjaya mantra. He also advised Markendeya to utter the mantra in the presence of Shiva.

Eventually, the end of 15th year approaches and Markendeya started his sacrifice to Lord Shiva in the form of *linga*. The dawn approaches and the boy reached his 16th year.

Markendeya realised in any moment Yama's servants will arrive to take him. In a hurry, Markendeya started to chant the death repellent mantra which was taught by Brahma, with his heart beating faster due to anxiousness.

As per told by fate, suddenly Markendeya saw few creatures were advancing towards him. The creatures were ugly with glowing red eyes; looking very fierce and their skin were dark like a heap of collyrium. Each of the weird and ugly looking creatures was holding a noose.

The ugly creatures suddenly stopped as if something was pushing them away from Markendeya. Surprised at this incident, the creatures spotted Markendeya chanting the Mahamrityunjaya Mantra which is the reason of repelling.

Clenching their jaws and frowning ferociously, one of the creatures said, "Markendeya, stop chanting the mantra, come to us as per your fate!"

"No, I will not come!" shouted Markendeya in return.

The creature turned to his master who seemed to be way bigger than the others.

"How master?" he asked confused.

"We are not powerful enough to dispel the mantra", the huge creature answered in a low growling voice.

"Let's go and submit this case to Lord Yama", he continued.

Without warning the creatures turned and vanished in blinding light. They returned to the netherworld and met Yama who was sitting on his throne made by human skulls. Yama upon seeing his servants "Where is Markendeya's soul?" asked Yama calmly upon seeing his servants walking towards him.

The huge creature which is the master choked back his voice and said, "My lord, the boy cannot be captured as he is chanting something."

"What do you mean?" frowned Yama standing.

"Yes, lord. The mantra seem to repel us and we have no the slightest idea about it", continued the creature.

"Hmm, it surely is the Mahamrityunjaya mantra…" murmured Yama slowly. The lord of death smiled and soon the smile turned into uproar of laughter. The creatures looked astonished.

"My lord, why are you laughing?" asked one of the creatures timidly. Yama stopped his laughter and answered, "The mantra that Markendeya is chanting is a death repellent mantra but it will not stop me!"

"I will go and capture his soul myself." snorted Yama. Taking his *danda* (noose), the god vanished.

The superintendent of death made way to Markendeya. Yama saw that the boy was doing sacrifices to Lord Shiva while chanting the death repellent mantra.

Yama quickens his pace towards Markendeya. Markendeya saw Yama rushing towards him. He quickly stopped chanting the Mantra and ran to Lord Shiva's *linga* and hugged it tightly.

Yama came in front of Markendeya who was hugging the *linga*, He laughed and said in a sarcastic tone, "You think Lord Shiva can save you?" Markendeya replied confidently, "Lord Shiva will save his devotees no matter how difficult the situation is!"

"Confident aren't you, boy" Yama smirked. "Now let's see if your lord can save you or not!", yelled Yama. Whirling his noose like a cowboy, the god threw the noose to Markendeya.

However, Markendeya ducked his head and the noose fell upon the *linga* of Lord Shiva.

Immediately, Lord Shiva himself rose from the *linga*, holding his trident. His eyes were reddish like hot copper. Seeing the lord of destruction in anger, Yama flinched.

"Yama, how dare you touch my devotee?" "Foolish!" "I will teach you a lesson you will not forget!"

Lord Shiva pulled Yama with the noose. As the supritendent of death stumble forward towards Lord Shiva, the god of destruction kicked him strongly on the chest. Yama flew backwards and he himself passed to the death kingdom.

Lord Shiva turned to Markendeya who looked terrified and said in gentle voice, "Markendeya, you are great devotee, so I bless you will live for sixteen aeons", saying so, the Lord disapeared.

Markendeya sighed after cheating death. Without any moment to lose he returned to his parents. Mrikandu was surprised that his son escaped death.

"Oh my God! You are alive!" exclaimed Mrikandu happily. Upon hearing Mrikandu's shouts, his wife stormed out of the kitchen.

"Oh Markendeya! Thank the gods, he is alive!" screamed his mother with great satisfaction. She hugged Markendeya tightly and was so ecstatic in her motherly feeling. Tears flow down her cheeks when she took him on her lap and began kissing his fragrant head; in affection she enjoyed the company of Markendeya.

"How can you escape death?" asked Mrikandu softly. Markendeya narrated what happened during the sacrifice, of how Yama and his hellish servants came to capture his soul and how Lord Shiva himself killed Yama.

"What?" "Yama is dead?" questioned Mrikandu quickly. "Yes Father, I saw with my own eyes, the Death himself lost his life" replied Markendeya picking up a bunch of juicy grapes and began to pop in his mouth.

Mrikandu kept silent for a while. 'Death is dead, people will not die anymore', he began to think. Not very long afterwards, a lady came running to his house.

"Why what is the matter, Shanti?" Mrikandu asked the woman, standing up. Markendeya followed his father's actions looking surprised.

"Sage, my husband was dead just moments ago, I confirm, but he is now had risen and is as normal as before", complained Shanti rubbing her sari drenched with perspiration.

"I think some demon took his body, please come and see it" "I am frightened!"

"Ok, do not worry, I will see to it", said Mrikandu, storming out of his hut, followed by Markendeya and the scared Shanti. They walked hurriedly to Shanti's hut which was located a stone's throw away.

Upon reaching her hut, Mrikandu and Markendeya saw a man sitting in a meditating posture. "Look at him, doesn't look like dead does he?", asked Shanti quietly.

Mrikandu ignored her and walked towards the man, "Sir, your wife said you died minutes ago, how are you back in this world?" The man opened his tightly shut eyes, "sage Mrikandu, it is true that I dropped dead but none of Lord Yama servants came to catch my soul. So, I didn't pass to the dead kingdom."

"Ok, it is puzzling," replied Mrikandu standing. He turned to Shanti who was standing at the doorstep, frightened. "It is ok, no demoniac being possessed your husband's body, It is your husband". Shanti breathed a great relief.

It is said that when the soul leaves this body, it must be destroyed. That is the reason why Hindus' burn the body after a person' death. If the body is not destroyed, the various demoniac beings will attempt to use the body for an evil purpose. The human body is nothing but a mixture of five gross elements namely; earth, fire, water, air and ether. The body serves as a cage for the immortal soul (*atman*). The soul cannot be destroyed but the body can. After the destruction of the body, the soul transmigrates to another body. The *Bhagavad-Gita* states that: As a person puts on new garments, giving up the old ones, the soul similarly accepts new body, giving up the old and useless ones. This is the process of rebirth and will continue to happen until the soul achieves *Mukthi* (liberation).

Mrikandu and Markendeya walked back to their hut. "Father, how can Shanti's husband not die?", asked Markendeya.

"I think since Lord Yama himself is dead, thus no one can die now", answered Mrikandu thoughtfully.

"Oh my god! This will cause imbalance in the universe", exclaimed Markendeya.

"I agree", replied his father.

"So, father what should be done?"

"I think you must pray to Lord Shiva to restore Yama. Only then, the balance can be restored".

Markendeya nodded. After all, it was due to him that Yama is dead. Now he must rectify the problem.

Markendeya rushed to Lord Shiva's temple. He came infront of Lord Shiva's statue in form of *linga*. Lord Shiva is usually worshipped in this form.

Standing humbly in front of *linga*, Markendeya bowed and sang:

There is nothing called as nonexistent!
Implied everthing exists in You
The material world and gross elements is all under You
Then, why this affection for me?
Is the legend about the phallic symbol of you testifying a lie?
Were your arguments in Lord's court a prevarication?

Carrying loads of sand on your head for food!
My Lord, you get flogged by sticks!
You are the master of this world!
Hence, why are you not responding the calls of your devotee??

Immediately, lightning flashed and Shiva himself with his trident emerged from the Linga.

Markendeya bowed. The lord blessed him. Markendeya said, "My lord, since you killed Yama to save me. People are not dying anymore. Please bring Yama back, so that people will continue to pass to the death kingdom and so that the balance of the world is restored".

"If so is your wish, I will bring back Yama", replied Shiva.

Markendeya bowed thankfully. Lord Shiva called, "Yama!". Immediately, the lord of death appeared as good as before. Yama flexed his fingrs, examinining his arms and straightened his shoulders. He saw Markendeya and Shiva gripping his great trident.

"Lord Shiva, you are the best of the gods. Please excuse me for trying to capture your devotee's soul. I am conscious about my mistake."

"It is alright Yama. Be assured that you can carry on with your duties now. But you must never disturb my devotees. Tell your servants too", said Lord Shiva gently but in a strict tone.

"Yes, my lord", said Yama bowing. Lord Shiva gestured the death god to return to his abode known as Yamaloka.

After this, Lord Shiva also vanished leaving Markendeya alone in the temple. Markendeya smiled and chanted, "Om Namo Sivaya!" and made way to his house feeling glad that the balance of the world will be restored.

NOTE:

The name Shanti used in this story is a fictionist name just for an identity purpose.

The Mahamrityunjaya mantra is a very confidential mantra. It is only known to Markendeya in the ancient times but now it is recorded in *Rig Veda, Yajur Veda* and *Atharva Veda*

THE IMPRISONEMENT OF LORD BRAHMA BY KUMARA

O nce upon a time, Lord Brahma was imprisoned by Lord Muruga for being ignorant about the fundamentals of creation and being prideful over his knowledge. This interesting tale is narrated here.

Once, Lord Brahma; the father of progenitors of the universe when he was moulding the ingredients of the creation came to a complete halt when he encountered unusual element.

"What is this, I have never seen this" said Brahma to himself surprised. "Hmm, I need to ask other god," continued Brahma. Brahma said slowly, "Lord Vishnu cannot be bothered with this petty stuff." He paused for a second, thinking hard. Suddenly he exclaimed, "Ya! I know, I will meet Lord Shiva, maybe he knows this."

"Sarasvati! I need to go Kailash regarding some affairs of cosmos," yelled Brahma top of his voice, rising from his golden throne.

"Yes dear, good luck in that," replied Sarasvati suddenly appearing beside her husband.

Brahma walked out of his place hurriedly and went to his mount which was a swan. The swan of Lord Brahma is not of ordinary type of swan that is found in this world. The swan of Lord Brahma is known as *parahamsa*. According to Bhaktivedanta Swami, the *parahamsa* has the capability of separating a mixture of milk and water by withdrawing the milk portion and rejecting the watery portion.

Brahma yoked the reins of his mount and in a flash it rose and vanished. The *parahamsa* travelled through the darkness of the universe and reached planet of Lord Shiva also known as Rudraloka.

Brahma directed his swan to the capital city of Rudraloka; the Kailash mountains which was covered by snow. The swan journeyed straight to the mountain peaks. It stopped abruptly and nearly sent Lord Brahma flying over.

The creator god scowled and got down his mount. The swan immediately went pecking some pebbles o the frozen ground. Lord Brahma adjusted his red splashed garments and entered the golden gates which was guarded by a pair of axe wielding ghanas who bowed to Brahma as he passed the gates. Lord Brahma ascends to the summit and in his journey he saw Lord Muruga practising his martial arts.

Seeing that the mountain god kicked a stone and the stone cracked, Brahma said, "Well! Well! Muruga, always kicking and punching I see."

Skanda turned his head and saw Brahma grinning from ear to ear as if his practices were same sort of performance. Nevertheless, Lord Muruga bowed and replied, "My Lord, I was just practising my moves."

"Hmmm," snorted Brahma, sitting on a rock and crossing his legs. Muruga kept silent at the creator's behaviour. 'Has he no respect?' thought Muruga angrily.

"So, I expect you have no knowledge regarding the universe matter?", questioned Brahma testily petting his legs. Muruga kept quiet but rage started to bloom in his heart.

Seeing the silence of the mountain god, Brahma snorted "Foolish god, aren't you!" and rose. Muruga's eye turned reddish as he saw Lord Brahma casually walking to the pathway to the summit.

"Hold on a second!" shouted Skanda, advancing to Brahma who face froze at Kumaran's command.

"What is it?" asked Brahma frowning.

"Since, you are very knowledgeable about the affairs of creation, I have a question to ask." whispered Muruga. "I have no time for silly question, Muruga," replied Brahma arrogantly.

"Please, Lord Brahma, just one question," pleaded Muruga pitifully. "Alright, but make it quick!" ordered Brahma without looking at Skanda's face.

"I want to know how you create?" asked Muruga. "This is your question? Well, I willcreate after I meditated to Lord Vishnu. Then He supplied the *Vedas*" answered Brahma easily. Muruga looked confused.

"Have I answered your question, Muruga?" asked Brahma seeing Kumara's confused face.

"One more question, my lord", said Muruga showing his index finger as a sign.

Lord Brahma sighed but he nodded. "Can you tell me one line from the *vedas* that you use to create?" asked Skanda.

"What for? Even if I tell you, it is way too high for you, you will never be able to understand" replied Brahma. "Don't worry about it; I just wanted to know a line"

"Hmmm, stubborn god you are. Alright let"s take an example from *Rig Veda*. It states that "Om......," Brahma stopped Lord Muruga halted him by carrying his palm just like a traffic police stops a vehicle on a road.

"What is it?" asked Brahma flabbergasted. "I want to know the meaning of Om that you uttered just now," replied Muruga clutching his Vel.

"Oh, that one...ah...Om...Om...Om" stammered Brahma while his hand started counting the prayer beads and his another hand started to rub the *vedas*.

"Yes! I am waiting!, I have to continue my practise!," said Muruga slightly annoyed.

"My dear Velava, I have no slightest idea about Om" answered Brahma miserably, nodding his four heads in desperation.

Immediately Lord Muruga jumped and with his strong hand like mountain, he knocked Lord Brahma on his head. Brahma saw Muruga's action like a flash and before he could say anything, his vision becomes blurred.

Holding his hand, Brahma suddenly sat down in pain. He looked up at Muruga who looked very angry.

Lord Muruga closed his eyes and murmured. Immediately a rope appeared in his hands. The mountain lord seized the dazed Brahma just like a lion seizes a deer and bound him with the ropes.

"Ahh, Muruga, what are you doing?" asked Brahma frightened as he saw Muruga binding him tighter and tighter.

"You do not know the meaning of Om and yet you brag in front of me that I have not enough knowledge," yelled Muruga, now putting a knot.

"I am sorry, my lord, in the pride of my knowledge, I mistook you as ignorant. Now I know I am ignorant." "Please Muruga, release me, I need to continue my duty to create"

"No way Brahmadeva, for your arrogance, I need to teach you a lesson so that the thought of you having supreme knowledge and underestimating other's potential will not be problem anymore!," shouted Muruga coming near to Brahma's frightened face.

Lord Muruga pulled the bound Brahma all the way to a prison cave. Reaching the cave, the lord pushed Brahma roughly into the prison through the steel bars. Brahma stumbled and fell into the prison, passing through the bars like an image.

Muruga grinned and suddenly walked away leaving Brahma shouting in desperation. Brahma walked to the bars and attempted to pass through it but failed and the god flung backwards. The prison bars are designed in such a way that it will allow prisoners in but not out.

Brahma sighed and sat on the cold floor in frustration. Having nothing to do, the god started to meditate. Brahma remained in the cell for quite some time and caused the process of creation come to halt.

Indra in the high heavens realised that the creation had stopped. "What is happening?!" thought Indra loudly. He gulped the Soma juice. Usually the intoxicant made him think, but not this time. Indra breathed deeply and called his brethrens, "Agni, Vayu, Varuna, Yama and others, come here at once!" The other gods received Indra's call. They vanished from their respective abodes and appeared in front of the confused Indra.

"Indra!, terrible things are happening, creation is not taking place!" said Agni, accidentally flicked his hand causing a luminous flame to erupt from his hand.

"Yes, I knew, that is the reason I called all of you" replied Indra rising from his throne and advancing to the gods. "Creation has stopped so I think something happened to Lord Brahma," suggested Yama intelligently.

"That is what I thought too," replied Indra in a hushed tone. "Ok, if we were presuming Brahma is absent, we must find out the cause," said Vayu in his windy voice.

"Hmmm, then there is only one way, we need to search for Brahma. Maybe he is playing hide and seek with Goddess Sarasvathi and grew careless about his duties" said Indra. Other other gods stared at him.

"Ok, just joking." mumbled Indra after he realised that no one laughed at his joke.

"I appreciate your efforts Indra, but we need to get going" interrupted Varuna. He is certainly did not want to hear any jokes in this times of trouble.

"Yes! You are right!" said Indra loudly. "I think we should start finding Lord Brahma in his abode." continued Devendra. The other gods nodded in agreement.

The gods vanished in blinding light and appeared in Brahmaloka. They entered the hall headed by Indra. "Mother, where is Lord Brahma?," asked Indra loudly after seeing the goddess of learning sitting on her throne looking very sad as if she lost something.

"I have no idea Indra, he went to Kailash regarding some affairs and he has not returned" answered Sarasvathi gesturing her hand to empty throne of Lord Brahma.

"Kailash......something happened to him" said Vayu quietly. "What?" questioned Sarasvathi suddenly lifting up her head. "Nothing ....." "We will search Kailash and bring him back," answered Indra quickly. They thanked Sarasvathi and disappeared.

The gods appeared directly in front of the gateway of Kailash Mountains.

"Ok, let's meet Lord Shiva," suggested Vayu wrapping his body with his arms. Indra nodded and they entered Kailash after paying respect to a pairs of ghanas when Yama suddenly stopped.

"Any of you saw Lord Brahma entering?", asked Yama pointing his club to one of the ghana.

"Yes Lord Brahma entered but he has not exited. Probably he vanished straight to his planet," replied the ghana. "No, he is not there "said Varuna. The ghana shrugged indifferently.

"He entered but not exited, it is puzzling," murmured Indra. His stomach did a backflip thinking what would happen to the creator.

The gods climbed the mountain and eventually came in front of Mahadeva who is meditating as his trident literally stood beside him.

"My Lord, we need your help. Please make time for us" said Indra bowing. Lord Shiva opened his eye and saw the assembly of gods standing in front of him. "Welcome Indra and others, what brought you to Kailash"

"My Lord, Brahma had disappeared and process of creation is not taking place," complained Agni.

"What?," Brahma is missing!?" "How can it be?" replied Lord Shiva suddenly rising and clutches his trident.

"We have no idea, it seems that Brahma had come to meet you," continued Indra hesitantly.

"Brahma had not met me," answered Lord Shiva slowly. The other gods looked flabbergasted. "Don't worry, I will handle this matter" said Lord Shiva, seeing the gods' frightened faces.

He closed his eyes for a moment and opened it. Smiling he said, "Brahma is in prison and I know who put him there." The gods looked at each other.

Varuna asked, "My Lord, who prisoned Brahma" "My son, Kumara did this," replied Lord Shiva and without any prior notice, he immediately vanished.

The gods sat on the snow covered floor. Vayu said angrily, "This mountain god is never rational, how can he imprison Brahma?" "Husshh!" cautioned Indra. "Muruga is the commander of devas and maybe Lord Brahma did something," he added. "Yes, it is not for us to judge Skanda's decision," continued Varuna.

Lord Shiva appeared in front of Muruga who was playing with his peacock carrier. The mountain god once saw his father, immediately bowed.

"Father, please accept my respect" said Muruga as his golden crown touching Lord Shiva's feet. "Stand up, Kumara," ordered Lord Shiva. Muruga rose. Lord Shiva looked sour.

"Why have you imprisoned Brahma?" "Have you no respect on how to treat someone older than you? "What the *Vedas* say about treating a guest?" questioned Lord Shiva angrily.

"Father, Brahma made a few mistakes" replied Skanda in a hurt tone.

"Hmmm, what mistakes?" asked Shiva suddenly growing soft.

"First, he disrespected me and when I asked about the meaning of Om, he could not answer" complained Muruga. "So, to teach him a lesson, I imprisoned him." continued Muruga.

"Hmmm, I see," said Shiva "You said Brahma do not know the meaning of Om. Well, do you?"

"Yes, father," answered Muruga clutching his Vel. "Tell me the meaning, my son" ordered Lord Shiva.

Muruga replied, "Father, I will tell the meaning of the supreme sound Omkara but with one condition."

"What is it", asked Shiva.

"I wanted you to accept me as teacher and I will tell the meaning" answered Muruga grinning.

"If so is your wish then its ok, I will be your student," replied Shiva amused.

"But, you need to release Brahma after this, is that clear?"

"Yes, father," answered Muruga.

Shiva let go his trident and it stood gleaming. The lord picked up his son in his arms just like a mother was to carry her child Muruga clasped his arm around his father's blue neck.

Lord Shiva, using his mystic power made a rock juts out from the snow covered ground. He let his son who sat on the rock smiling beautifully. Lord Shiva himself sat on the ground.

In this way, we understand since Lord Shiva accepted Muruga as a teacher, so Muruga must sit on a higher position signifying that he is a teacher and since Shiva is a student, he cannot sit on a position higher or equal to a teacher, so he simply sat on the ground. In other words the system of receiving knowledge is fully understood and applied by Shiva and Muruga.

"Ok, son, I am ready" said Lord Shiva humbly. Muruga at once began to import the knowledge of the supreme sound Om to his father.

Om is nothing but the manifestation of Lord Vishnu. From Om, the creation emanates. Bhaktivedanta Swami explained that the supreme sound Omkara is one of the different representation of Lord Krishna (Krishna is Vishnu and Vishnu is Krishna). That is the reason why almost all the hymns to the gods start with Om. However, for Lord Vishnu, the hymn starts with the word 'Hare'. Hare means Vishnu. This is the significance that Vishnu is beyond everthing. The universal mantra is Om, but the creator of Omkara is none other than Lord Vishnu.

After receiving the knowledge regarding the supreme sound, Lord Shiva thanked Muruga and reminded him to release Brahma.

After saying so, the lord vanished and appeared in front of gods. "I have solved this, Kumara will release Brahma soon, please go back to your duties" said Lord Shiva closing his eyes, entering the meditation world.

"Thank you Lord!" exclaimed the gods. Bowing, they returned to their own abodes in this universe.

Lord Muruga appeared in front of the meditating Brahma in the prison. "Open your eyes, Brahma, I have forgiven you." "Now you are released, please return to your abode" said Muruga softly.

Brahma opened his eyes, looking at Muruga, he bowed, "Kumara, due to my knowledge, I had become ignorant. But you taught me a lesson that can never be forgotten. Thank you" said Brahma. Kumara nod his head.

Brahma who is the master of this universe, circambulated Lord Kartikeya three times was ready to return to his planet of residence. The mountain god gestured him, giving him the permission to return.

NOTE:

Since Lord Shiva behaved like a student to Lord Muruga, thus giving the name Swaminatha Swami to Lord Muruga. Swamimalai temple which is located in India is the actual place where this tale took place.

THE DELIVERANCE
OF THE DEMON LORD RAVANA

The great Hindu epic known as Ramayana narrates about the heroic struggle of Lord Rama against the powerful demon king; Ravana to free Sitadevi. This epic was written by the sage Valmiki and is slightly modified by a Tamil poet, Kamban.

Ravana is not an ordinary demon. He has ten heads and obtained boon from Lord Brahma that he cannot be killed by any beings except humans. The reason is that he kept a pot of nectar of immortality *(amrita)* in his stomach.

After obtaining the boon, Ravana went to conquer all beings in this universe. His son is the great Indrajit (conquerer of Indra). Indrajit conquered the heaven and drove out King Indra. Ravana also conquered hell but appointed his brother, Abhiravana as the king.

Ravana established his kingdom known as Lanka; an island separated by sea. Lanka originally belongs to Kubera (god of riches), but forcefully taken by Ravana. His kingdom is still existent today and it is now modern Sri Lanka.

Not many people knew that Ravana even tried to attack Kailash, to conquer Lord Shiva. The tale is narrated here;

Ravaneswara, after conquering all the places in this universe and establishing his great kingdom; Lanka (now modern day, Sri Lanka), expressed his new intentions to his ministers. He said, "Dear ministers of Lanka, I wish to conquer Kailash. What is your opinion?"

"Oh great Lankesh, we think that nothing in this universe can be compared to you, we believe that everything is under you. Thus, Kailash remains as the final place that you haven't conquered. So, if you ask our opinion, we think that conquering Kailash is a good idea", one of his demonic minister said enthusiastically.

"Yes, what you said is the truth. I will travel to Kailash and conquer it as soon as possible", replied Ravana feeling encouraged.

He rose from his throne and said in a thunderous voice "Minister!" "Yes, my lord?"

"Guard Lanka defensively, I am going to Kailash now. Let me return with victory!" said Ravana loudly

"Your wish, my lord, I will guard Lanka with my life," the minister replied. The great demon stormed out, walking in midst of his ministers out of from the hall and boarded his vehicle known as *pushpaka-vimana*. The *pushpaka-vimana* is a flying chariot which is capable of travelling at very speed and has the ability to change its shape.

Ravana yoked his chariot and in a blink of an eye, it rose to the sky and in a second, lost from the vision of the minister.

Ravana rode the *pushpaka-vimana* to the space and travel beyond human speculation. He crossed many planets and eventually came to his destination; Rudraloka.

Rudraloka is the planet of Lord Shiva whereas Kailash is the capital city where Lord Shiva and his associates live. Kailash is a range of silver mountains covered by snow.

Without wasting any time, Ravana landed his *pushpaka-vimana* at the entrance and then he proceeded on foot to the entrance. The cold air seemed to have no effect on the demon. His purpose was that he wanted to conquer Kailash with diplomatic approach first.

Walking towards the entrance, Ravana saw that the entrance was guarded by Nandisvara; the eternal companion of Lord Shiva.

"All hail to Nandisvara, the eternal companion of Lord Shiva, permit me to enter." shouted Ravana loudly extending his strong arms as a sign of respect.

"Who are you mortal being to seek entrance into Kailash!" "Name yourself!" Nandi ordered, pointing his index finger to the demon king.

"You don't know me? You fool! I am the great Ravana, the conquerer of the three worlds"

"Now, let me enter", replied Ravana in a very strong voice, ordering Nandi.

"Ravana, Lord Shiva is now meditating and he will not see anyone at this time. Please return", answered the white bull gently.

"Don't be dumb, Shiva will see me as I am his great devotee"

"No, please return"

"Shut up, no one talks to me like that, you are just an animal and you won't know about this, let me enter or I will turn ferocious"

"Don't tempt me!", said Ravana angrily.

He closed his eyes and murmured some magic words. Suddenly, out of nowhere, two heads begin to appear side by side from his original head and continue to expand till the total heads are now 10 in number. In short Ravana looked like a mutant alien with multiple heads. Each head begin to roar to scare Nandi away.

Nandi felt no fear at the sight of Ravana's frightening appearance which will surely cause any human to die of heart attack.

The white bull felt slightly annoyed to see the demon that refused to listen to him. Thus, rage flooded into Nandi's heart. Nandisvara; the eternal companion of Shiva said in very grave voice full of anger, "Ravana, because of your stupidity and arrogance, I strongly curse you that Lanka will be destroyed by an army of bears and apes," This curse proved effective when Lord Rama attacked Ravana with an army of apes and bears. This is also the ultimate reason why Lanka was destroyed in that siege.

"Your curse is ineffective to me!" one of the ten heads of the demon king said in a strong and arrogant voice. The other nine heads of Ravana cackled in laughter.

"You don't permit me to enter, so now you shall witness my love for Shiva!" yelled Ravana pointing his index finger which was decorated with enormous ring to Nandi. "I shall uproot this Kailash mountain and disturb his meditation", he continued.

Ravana closed his eyes for a moment. All of a sudden, ten hands begin to sprout of his muscular body. He roared as if the hands gave him super strength which proved to be true. Ravana made his way towards Nandi who was guarding the gates and pushed Nandi roughly. The white bull flew and landed three feet away with a thud.

Ravana slid his hands (ten of them) into the base of the snow capped mountain exactly like a person slips his hands into the pockets. Satisfied that his hands successfully entered deep into the base of the mountain, Ravana roared like a lion and carried it. His mighty muscles ripped as Kailash was carried upon a demon's back.

In the start, the enormous weight of the entire mountain dropped on Ravana's back, almost smashing him flat until he managed to get on his powerful knees. With great difficulty, Ravana supported Kailash just like a schoolboy carrying his backpack.

Nandisvara got to knees just as the moment, Ravana carried the mountain. The white bull gaped open at the demon's action.

"You see this Nandi! See?" shouted Ravana under the mountain. "No one is more powerful than me in this universe!!!!" he yelled at the top of his lungs.

"Ravana, you foolish demon, you have made a great mistake!" replied Nandi gazing at the peak where Lord Shiva resides.

"What do you mean, Nandi? I have done no mistake! I am only exhibiting my great power, to Shiva", answered Ravana. Nandi kept quiet hearing Ravana's reply. He understood that this demon become very puffed up with his powers.

Bhaktivedanta Swami explained that when demons become very powerful, they defy the gods. They wanted to go against the laws of gods. Any intelligent personality knows very well that the purpose of god cannot be violated and there is no one is ever successful in doing so. However, this kind of realization is never attainable by these so called materially powerful men and demons such as Ravana, Surapadman.

Lord Shiva is the lord of this material universe. The three modes of material nature namely passion, goodness and ignorance are under the subjugation of Shiva. Thus, among the gods, Lord Shiva is known as Mahadeva (greatest god), practically because he is the master of this universe and the god of destruction. However, this demon Ravana has particularly forgotten that Mahadeva is clearly not some other minor gods that he previously conquered.

Ravana then shook the entire mountain with his great profound strength. Kailash swayed like a blade of grass being subjected to strong wind.

Shiva, who was meditating on the peak of the mountain, opened his eyes and he rose from his seat. Mahadeva gripped his great trident. His face turned sour and his eyes turned reddish like fire burning. Shiva used his mystic power and he saw that Ravana is responsible for this entire commotion.

Deciding to teach Ravana a lesson, the lord pressed his littlest toe on the mountain. The force was so great until the mountain started to descend on Ravana who desperately tried to hold it in the initial position.

"Ahh... what is this?!" Ravana screamed.

"And why I can't move it" cried Ravana loudly. The loudness of Ravana's scream was so great until it is written in the great epic Ramayana, that it shook the heavens and earth. This is also when the demon king got his name of 'Ravana'.

"Come here ghana," called Shiva to one of the ghana there. The ghana obediently walked and said "Lord, what you want me to do?"

Lord Shiva answered in a powerful voice, "I want you to go to Ravana and inform him that he disturbed my meditation, so I pinned him under this mountain."

"I will carry out your wish immediately,", answered the ghana respectfully and quickly hurried to Ravana who was still crying loudly due to the enormous weight of Kailash. The ghana said, "O Ravana, you had foolishly disturbed Lord Shiva's penance and as a punishment the Lord pinned this mountain under you.

"Thank you for telling me the situation. I do realise my mistake now", said Ravana remorsefully his head drooping like sad dog. After a moment, he continued, "Please return to Shiva and permit me to undergo my punishment".

"My dear Lord Shiva; the greatest of demigods, even if you had pinned me under this Kailash mountain, I can still praise you!" screamed Ravana. Saying so, the ruler of Lanka plucked his own nerves and ties them together to form a collection of strings. He then tied the collection of strings to his *veena* which he carried everywhere. The demon lord then started to strum the nerves on his *veena* and at the same time he sang praises to Lord Shiva.

Ravana is one of the greatest *veena* players. The demon lord is so expert in playing *veena* until he also used the *veena* as a symbol on his flag.

Legend give us the information that Ravana sang praises about Lord Shiva for many years until Lord Shiva took away his littlest toe thus releasing Ravana from the mountain. The collective songs and praises that Ravana sang to Lord Shiva are collectively known as Shiva Tandava Stotra. After hearing the praises by Ravana, Shiva grew compassionate to his devotee and he removed his toe.

Ravana at once felt that the weight of Lord Shiva's toe is removed. Feeling relieved, Ravana dropped back the mountain to the original place after escaping.

He stood in front of the tall mountain and murmured, "Om Namo Shivaya!" Lord Shiva disappeared from his place of meditation and appeared in front of Ravana. Ravana immediately bowed to the lord. He said "O supreme Lord Shiva; Mahadeva, I realised my mistake and please accept my apology"

The god replied "Ravana, I am happy to hear your praises. For your unalloyed devotion, I give you my personal weapon". Shiva extends his hand and in an eye blink a curved sword appears in his palm. Lord Shiva handed him the curved sword.

"This is *Chandrahas*, this weapon is extremely powerful, but beware if you were to use this sword against wrong people, the sword will return to me and your days will be numbered". Shiva explained.

Ravana replied, "Thank you my Lord for this wonderful sword; bless me that you will protect me"

"So be it, Lanka will be a great kingdom under you" blessed Lord Shiva. This blessing of Lord Shiva to Ravana proved true that under Ravana's rule, the kingdom Lanka flourished and it was said that even the house of poorest person in Lanka had golden pots which stocked grains. In short there was no starvation in his kingdom.

After obtaining the blessings of the Lord, Ravana returned to Lanka with *pushpaka vimana*. He was a great devout to Lord Shiva and had successfully obtained his grace although Ravana is a demon.

NOTE:

The tale of the demon lord, Ravana lifting Mount Kailash and Lord Shiva pinning him underneath is a popular tale. This form of Lord Shiva is known as Ravananugraha which is a benevolent aspect of Lord Shiva.

THE FEUD BETWEEN LORD GANESHA AND LORD KARTIKEYA

Once upon a time in Kailash Mountains, Lord Shiva and his consort, Parvathi was sitting on their thrones. They were listening to some songs and dances by their devotees. All of them were feeling very jubilant and happy.

Suddenly, Lord Shiva turned his head towards Parvathi and asked, "My dear, where are Ganesh and Kartikeya?"

"They were playing over there," answered Parvathi pointing her index finger to the northern direction.

"Hmm, ok," replied Shiva and turned his attention to the performance.

All of a sudden, Lord Shiva and Parvathi heard the chanting of, 'Narayana'. Lord Shiva smiled while Parvathi looked worried as the great sage Narada entered their residence, carrying the *veena*.

Shiva held up his hand and the performance stopped abruptly. The dancers and devotees moved away from the place. Narada walked towards the lord. Narada is a great saint, his hair dazzled like molten gold and his aura was emanating from his body scattered in all directions.

"All glories to Lord Shiva and Parvathi! Please accept my greetings," said Narada, folding his hands and bowing his head as a sign of respect. Shiva and Parvathi held their right hand and blessed him.

Shiva then enquired, "Narada why have you come here?" The three-eyed god sensed something mischievous going on the sage's mind but he did not say anything. Narada loves to stir up troubles among the gods but ultimately the trouble will end in a good way, restoring truth (*Dharma*)

"My dear Lord Shiva, I have obtained a magical fruit. It bestows the consumer eternal knowledge and great intelligence as it was blessed by gods and various sages," replied Narada, taking out a golden mango from his robes. The mango shone brilliantly like gold.

Narada held the greatly prized mango with his both hands and in great care, he hand in over to the god of destruction on his throne. Lord Shiva took the fruit from Narada hands.

"Thank you, Narada," replied Shiva and he used his mystic power to summon a knife. Suddenly, a bright sharp knife appeared in his hands. Holding the knife, Lord Shiva swung his knife but stopped in midair as Narada shouted, "No, lord, please don't cut the mango!"

Lord Shiva narrowed his eye. "What is the matter, Narada?" he asked surprised. Narada answered, "Lord, the mango must not be divided as it will lose its magical properties. This fruit of knowledge must be consumed as whole to gain its benefit."

Lord Shiva pressed his lips upon hearing the words of Narada. "If you say so... Parvathi, you should take this mango," he instructed his consort gently. Parvathi had no other choice than to receive the fruit from her husband.

"Good!" exclaimed Shiva as Parvathi took the mango from his hand. She held the mango, looking mystified and innocent. Narada also waited for her to consume the fruit but she did not do so. Lord Shiva turned his head to his consort and said, "What are you waiting for? Eat the mango, will you?"

Parvathi widened her eyes and replied innocently, "My dear, how can I consume something that you have not consumed? I will not eat this mango, take it back Narada,"

Narada waved his hand and replied, "The gift cannot be taken, mother."

"How lord?" pleaded Parvathi.

Parvathi had demonstrated the perfect example of being a wife. Actually after the husband took his food then only the wife will eat. A wife should never eat anything if the husband had not eaten. However this practice is not practiced now.

Hearing the pleas of his consort and quite agitated about Narada's plan, Lord Shiva said, "If none of us can have this mango, it is better for our children to consume it."

Breathing deeply, Parvathi replied, "That is a very good idea, *swami*." The word '*Swami*' means husband or Lord. According to Vedic rules, husband is equivalent to Lord. From this Sanskrit word 'Swami', comes the Malay word of 'suami'. It also means husband.

Lord Shiva held up his right and called loudly, "Ganesha, Muruga, come here at once!" In a blink of an eye, the brothers, namely Lord Ganesha and Lord Muruga appeared in front of their parents. They also saw Narada and immediately greeted the sage as a sign of respect. Narada blessed them.

"Father, why have you summoned us?" asked Ganesha humbly folding his hands.

"Narada brought a fruit of knowledge and gave it to me, but your mother and I have decided that this mango should be given to any of you," told Lord Shiva.

"But father, why can't you divide the mango? I think it is fairer" enquired Kartikeya. "It seems that the mango must be eaten as whole, if it is divided, the magical properties of this mango will be lost," explained Parvathi representing her husband.

"Oh, if that is the case, the mango should be given to me as I am the eldest child," said Ganesha quickly patting his stomach with his hands like a drum.

"I don't think so, brother, the mango should be mine as I am the youngest and you as the elder brother must compromise," said Kartikeya.

The two brothers soon began to quarrel to own the mango. Lord Shiva and Parvathi looked upon each other alarmed. Narada, however smiled mischievously. Shiva said in an annoyed voice, "Narada, have you served your purpose in causing trouble?"

"Shiva! Shiva!" replied the sage. "I didn't intend for this to happen," he continued.

"What to do, my dear?" asked Parvathi looking at her two sons, still fighting. "I think we must organise a competition and whoever win this competition shall get this fruit of knowledge," replied Lord Shiva looking at Parvathi.

"My dear, you are an expert in conducting competitions and trials, why don't you yourself suggest a good competition," replied Parvathi.

What Parvathi said about Lord Shiva is a fact. Lord Shiva loves to conduct tests, tribulations and competitions for his devotees.

From these he will get the pleasure. That is the reason the games of Lord Shiva is known as *Thiruvilayadal.*

Lord Shiva smiled and called in an authoritative tone, "Ganesha, Muruga, stop fighting and come here at once." Upon hearing their father's summon, the brothers stopped quarrelling and obediently came in front of Shiva.

"Vinayaka, Velava, I have decided that whoever can circulate the earth in the shortest time possible will have this mango," instructed the Lord.

As soon as Muruga heard the rules of the competition, he said confidently, "I will do it!" and smiled gleefully at his brother, hurried off to mount his vehicle which is a peacock.

Looking at his brother's action, Ganesha looked at his own body stature and said to himself, "My belly is enormous while my legs are stubby, so to circulate the world on my feet is out of the question. Hmm, my *vahana*; a mouse cannot surpass the speed of Kartikeya's peacock. How to win this competition?" he further asked in his own mind. Lord Shiva and Parvathi looked at each other upon seeing their eldest son's action.

"Narada, please come here," Ganesha called upon the sage Narada who immediately climbed the stairs and came in front of the elephant god. Bowing, the sage said respectfully, "Yes, Lord".

"Tell me Narada, what is the meaning of parents and what is the meaning of world," asked Lord Ganesha.

Astonished at the elephant god's question, Narada answered confidently, "Parents are the world and the world itself is equal to parents".

"True!, just wanted to confirm", replied Lord Ganesha happily.

"Father, mother, please stand together", said Ganapathi.

Lord Shiva and Parvathi looked at each other, confused but nevertheless stood together. Lord Ganesha smiled and touched his parents' legs and circumambulated them three times. No one could understand the purpose of Lord Ganesha, not even the great three eyed god and Parvathi. Everyone looked confused and flabbergasted.

Finishing his third round of circumambulating his parents, Lord Vinayaka, promptly took the prized fruit of knowledge from his mother's hand.

"Vinayaka, how can you obtain the fruit as you have not even circulated the earth." questioned Parvathi.

"Mother, I had been circulated the earth not once but thrice", replied Vinayaka. Lord Shiva and Parvathi exchanged surprised look.

"And how you can say that", asked Lord Shiva.

"Father, it is stated in the *Vedas* that parents are the representation of world. So, if I were to circulate both of you, am I not circulating the Earth?" explained Ganesha solemnly.

What Lord Ganesha said about the importance of parents is factual and is confirmed in various Vedic literatures. The Lord by his actions explained to the world that no being is of a higher position than parents. A saying proved this- *Matha* (mother), *Pitha* (father), *Guru* (teacher), *Deivam* (gods). According to level of importance in numerical order, mother is the most important followed by father and teacher. Finally are gods. A person must respect them in order to be successful in life. We must remember that without parents, we cannot come into this world. Bhaktivedanta Swami stated that due a father's mercy, one gets this material body. Thus father is considered as the first and foremost spiritual master. Without respecting and carrying out their orders, one cannot afford to be respected and after quitting this body, he may put in hellish conditions of life.

Upon hearing the clever comments from his son, Lord Shiva smiled. Raising his chest and his voice as grave as thundercloud, the great lord said, "My dear son, you have exceeded the expectations by portraying that parents are of the most important and certainly they are equivalent to earth. I believe that you are most eligible to receive this fruit".

Lord Ganesha immediately bowed to his father, received the mango. Smiling he turned to Parvathi, who was looking worried. Upon seeing her mother's expression, Vinayaka questioned gently, "O mother, why you look so worried?" "What bothers you?"

Parvathi replied in a very worried voice, "I do not think that Kartikeya will accept defeat".

"But Ganesha won the competition, what is the problem?" asked Lord Shiva gripping his trident tighter,

"I have no idea, my instinct is warning me something is going to happen", replied Parvathi looking worried.

At that moment, Kartikeya entered the hall, walking speedily and holding his *Vel*. Upon seeing the fruit of knowledge in the hands of Ganesha, he stopped abruptly. Tilting his body sideways, the lord of the mountains raised his voice and asked, "How is it possible that my brother can get this fruit? I don't think that he have circulated Earth faster than me".

Narada who was standing immediately replied, "Your brother had circumambulated the Earth not once but three times, and according to the rules of the competition, he is eligible to get the fruit of knowledge"

Muruga's eye dilated and in anger he turned to his mother who looked very worried, "Tell me mother, how is this possible", asked the mountain lord angrily.

"Vinayaka circulated us thrice and took the fruit from my hand. He said that parents are the world, so if he were to circulate us thrice, it means he had circulated the world", explained Parvathi looking straight to her second son's sour face.

After hearing the words of his mother, Lord Muruga raised his chest and spoke in a very powerful voice, "O both of you, have decided that eldest son is of more important, so all of you have acted very well. Well, that's it; I am leaving Kailash now as I am not respected here."

"Please Muruga, this is just a competition and you do not need to be angry for this matter, please don't leave us", pleaded Parvathi.

"No! Since I am not wanted here, I am leaving and don't expect me to change my decision. Goodbye!" replied Muruga, turning his back on his parents.

"Wait, Kartikeya, don't take harsh decision and please listen to your mother", Lord Shiva instructed strictly.

"I will not listen to anyone and I am leaving", answered Muruga angrily and he vanished from the sight leaving his parents and brother flabbergasted.

The mountain god appeared at the entrance of Kailash. Holding his celebrated *Vel*, he looked behind at the snow capped mountains, he snorted and walked hurriedly at the steps which was frozen with snowflakes.

Clutching his *Vel* tighter, Muruga continued descending the steps which led him away from his home. His face was sour and anger raged like a hurricane within his heart. At the same time, Lord Shiva and Parvathi looked upon each other. Parvathi exclaimed in a pitiful voice, "My dear lord, why is this happening? Why Muruga is so angry until he wanted to leave us?"

"Your son resolves to show that he is better than his brother and when he failed to do that, anger clouds his mind, preventing him from thinking rationally" answered Shiva not looking upon Parvathi's face. "Then, please bring him back." said Parvathi sobbing.

Lord Shiva turned his head towards Parvathi and without saying anything, he vanished with a puff of smoke. Shiva appeared a metre away from the angry Muruga who was descending the steps. Skanda saw his father and yet he crossed Lord Shiva and continued climbing down the steps.

Parvathi also tried to stop her son from leaving but is futile. Finally as a last attempt, Ganesha stood at the exit of Kailash holding the fruit of knowledge. When his younger brother came into sight, "Take this fruit, brother. Please don't leave us!" said Ganesha offering the fruit of knowledge. However Kartikeya does not care. He ignored his brother and exited the borders of Kailash. Skanda walked towards his peacock mount which was pecking some pebbles and mounted on the animal.

At once when Muruga mounted on the beast, the peacock screeched and rose into the air. Muruga made his way to a mountain on earth.

Dressed in only loincloth covering his pubic area, and armed with a stick, the mountain lord stood angrily on the summit of the mountain. This form of Muruga is called as the 'Aandhi Murugan'. The word Aandhi means devoid of anything. Thus Lord Skanda's form on the mountain is known as 'Murugan without anything'.

Muruga stood over the mountains for quite some time. During this period an old hermit by the name of Avvai came to know that her favourite god is angry with his parents. Attempt to cool him down, she made her way to the mountain and saw the mountain god devoid of anything.

"My dear Muruga, why have you forsaken your parents and come over here without anything?" asked Avvai looking at Muruga who is standing like a statue.

"My dear Avvai, my parents seem to put my elder brother as more important by giving him the fruit of knowledge", answered Kartikeya in a disappointed voice

"How can they do this, I have circulated the earth as they wanted but my brother won the fruit by his usual tricks" continued Muruga gripping his pole tightly.

Avvai listened to his lamentations patiently. After some time, she voiced out, "My dear Nyanapanditah, you yourself is a wisdom fruit. Why you want another wisdom fruit for? This is not right, lord. You of all gods taught me that parents are the first being to give importance, how can you be angry with them".

"No matter what happens, Avvai, I will stay here!!" said Muruga stubbornly.

Avvai started to sing a song to cool him down. She sang:

You are the wisdom fruit!!
You are Tamil's wisdom fruit!!
You enlightened even the assembly of scholars,
You emitted as a blaze from Lord Shiva's forehead,
You sprang up from six sacred lotuses,

You suckled from the Karthigai girls,
Your sacred fame is an admix of the universal mother hug,
Tamil wisdom fruit!!
You have repute, a place and a clan,
You have comforts, kin group and parents too,
You have an abode in Kailash Mountains where nimbus clouds dance,
Your mother has right intents,
Your father is passionate,
Mount on your peacock,
Seek out the lord!
Come and show up your grinning face!
Lord will accept you,
I will take you with me,
Come along!!

"Whatever you say, Avvai but I will continue to stay here", insisted Kartikeya frowning. Avvai knew that no one could change the mountain god's mind. Muruga is as stubborn as a mountain.

"It is alright, my lord. If you wanted to stay here and enact a play, who can stop you?"

"But I assure you that the next time I was to see you; you will be with your parents. This is for sure. I will take my leave now", says Avvai and vanished from the sight.

After the vanishing of Avvai, Parvathi Devi suddenly appeared in order to cool her son's anger. The goddess climbed the rocky stones of the mountain and saw her son standing on the peak wearing only a loincloth. Her heart grieved suddenly to see her son's condition.

"Muruga, there is no need to be angry. Come, let's go home", said Parvathi gently placing her hand on Kartikeya's shoulder. "No way am I coming home! All of you had made your stand that I am not important, so why should I return?" asked Muruga in a loud voice.

"My dear Muruga, this all are your father's games. For this small thing you are greatly disturbed," "Did you know that over the ages, your father enacts plays and games?"

"I will tell you some of his stories if you want", said Parvathi gently. "I am not prepared to hear anything, mother!" yelled Muruga.

"Don't say like that, I am sure that after you hear some of his tales, your rage will subside", replied Parvathi.

Muruga snorted but Parvathi started upon her first tale regarding Lord Shiva's games. After hearing few of his father's play, anger that bloomed in Skanda's heart subsided.

Lord Shiva who was meditating in Kailash at once sensed that his son's anger had subsided. The lord stood gripping his trident, vanished and appeared beside Parvathi on the mountain.

"So, Muruga, have you cooled down?" asked Shiva gently.

"Father, please forgive me, unknowingly I had become angry," pleaded Skanda bowing to his father.

"No worries, my son. Since you came here because of a fruit, from this day onwards, this mountain will be named as Palani and it will be a holy place of remembrance of this incidence to your devotees.", replied Shiva.

"Not only that, since you stood on this mountain summit with rage, let all the mountains will be worshipped as an abode of Kumaran hereafter by the entire world", said Parvathi. Muruga bowed his head to his parents.

"Mahadeva! Mahadeva!" boomed a voice suddenly. The air shimmered and Avvai appeared holding her stick and gazing up to the gods. The gods looked at Avvai in interest.

"Muruga your appearance along with your parents makes me feel happy. Instead of this, you stood alone". "I fear that the verse that I penned telling that 'Parents are the foremost of all gods' will be proved wrong by your actions." "Instead you gave life to the verse, I praise you whole heartedly". Muruga smiled hearing her praises.

"Old Tamil lady!!" called Lord Shiva suddenly. Avvai looked upon the Lord. "Throughout the world, you have done service to Tamil language", he continued. "O Altruist mother, honey of Tamil language!, Long live your Tamil", blessed the Lord.

"Now, tell me, what you consider as the unethical code of conduct?" asked Lord Shiva suddenly.

"Anything that does not pertain to the ethical life of a householder is unethical", answered Avvai.

"Well said!! What do you consider as good?" questioned Parvathi. "Worshipping at temples", said Avvai.

"Who is the learned person?" asked Parvathi testily. "Goddess, what is learnt is equivalent to what is held in the fist, but what is yet to be learnt is of the size of this world".

"Hahaha!!!" laughed Lord Shiva. "Very well said, Avvai!!" he continued.

"My dear Avvai, praise the Lord in numerical ascending order", instructed Parvathi. Nodding her head, Avvai sang:

You are single,
But in the body you are dual,

In the Tamil that evolved, you are a trinity,

In the virtuous tenents, you are a quartet,

In the verse 'NamaSivaya', you are a pentad,

In the gustory perception, you are a hexed,

In musical notes, you are a heptad,

In rumination, you are an octad,

You are a cherubic enneaded gem,

You are a tenner and beloved,

You are the begetter of the twelve handed Velavan,

You are the prime, the origin and has no ends,

You are equidistant from the former and the latter,

You stood as a duple of man and woman,

You said that they have equal status,

Half of your body is Uma,

You bestowed an equal half to woman,

You circulated as air,

You flared as blaze,

You beamed as light,

You became a source of water,

You are the past, present and eternal,

You burst as spring and radiate your warmth!!!

"Avvai, you Tamil and its flavour, you voice and its melody, your words and its connotations, it's in depth meanings, have all made me happy." "Long live your Tamil knowledge!" congratulated Lord Shiva.

"Thank you lord", replied Avvai closing her eyes and bowing her head in respect. When she opened her eyes, the gods have vanished.

V. Satish

Smiling and chanting, "Om Namo Sivaya!" Avvai made her way back to her hut which was located nearby feeling satisfied that Muruga had returned to his parents.

NOTE:

The Mountain Palani is one of Lord Muruga's holy shrines in India. Palani means fruit. Since the Lord stood on the mountain because of a fruit, the mountain is named Palani.

GLOSSARY

- Aabhirami Pattar – A devotee of Aadhi Sakthi
- Aadhi Sakthi – The primeval energy that emanates from the supreme sound; Omkara. Manifested in this material nature.
- Aarumugham – Six faces. Another name of Muruga
- Absolute Truth – The original truth whereby the material creation emanates; refers to Lord Vishnu
- Aditi – Mother of the demigods, wife to sage Kasyapa and the sister to Diti
- Aditya – Demigods, offsprings of Aditi
- Agnideva – The firegod
- Airvata – The albino elephant of Indra
- Amaravati – Capital city of the heavenly kingdom which was guarded by Airvata; Indra's albino elephant
- Ananta Sesa – An expansion of Vishnu. Multihooded snake which Lord Vishnu resides on.
- Anjana – A Vaanara. Mother of Hanuman. Wife of Kapiraja Kesari.
- Atmarama – Self satisfied. Refers to Vishnu and his incarnations
- Avvai – A renowed Tamil poet
- Ayodya – The kingdom of King Dasaratha where Lord Rama and Lakshmana appear.

- Badrikashama – Place of dwelling of Nara-Narayana
- Balarama – The incarnation of Anantadeva. Elder brother of Lord Krishna
- Bhagavad Gita – Spiritual instructions given by Lord Krishna to His friend Arjuna on the battlefield of Kurukshetra.
- Bhagavata Purana – Known as, 'Divine Eternal Tales of Supreme God'. One of the Puranic text of Hinduism with its focus on religious devotion to Supreme God Vishnu. The greatest and the purest of all Puranas. Also known as Maha- Purana.
- Bhaktivedanta Swami – The founder of International Society of Krishna Consciousness (ISKCON) and a great Vaishnava philosopher
- Bharatanatyam – Divine dance performed by Lord Shiva.
- Bhrigumuni – One of the mind sons of Lord Brahma. Revered as the most powerful sage
- Bhumi devi- earth goddess
- Brahma – Son of Lord Vishnu and the creator of the universe and the inhabitants
- Brahma Samhita – Ancient prayers of Lord Brahma offered to his father, Lord Vishnu in the beginning of the creation.
- Brahmajyoti – The effulgence that emanates from the body of Lord Vishnu
- Brahmaloka – The abode of Lord Brahma and is the highest planet in the material universe.
- Brihaspati – Advisor of King Indra, very knowledgeable; also known as Guru.
- Chandra – Moon God

- Chandradas – The personal sword of Lord Shiva which is shaped like a crescent moon. It means moon smile.
- Daitya – Demons, offsprings of Diti
- Dantavakra – King of Karusa. Wanted to avenge the death of Salva (his friend) by Lord Krishna but met his end in the hands of Lord Krishna.
- Dasaratha – Father of Rama, Lakshmana, Bharata and Satruguna
- Dashaavathar – Ten incarnations of Lord Vishnu.
- Dasyu- fortress of Vritra
- Devas – Demigods or gods numbering 33 million
- Devendra – Indra of the Devas. Another name of Indra
- Diti – Mother of demons, wife to Sage Kasyapa and the sister to Aditi
- Durga – The personification of this material universe. Incarnation of Parvathi. The younger sister of Lord Vishnu.
- Dvapara yuga – Third age of mankind
- Dvaraka – City of Lord Krishna.
- Eashenputra – Lord Ganesha. Eahsen means Shiva and putra means son. It means Son of Shiva
- Four Kumaras' – The first beings created by Brahma. They are the quardlet brothers namely Sanaka, Sanantana, Sananda and Sanat-kumara.
- Ganaphathi – Lord Ganesha. Meaning Lord of the Ghanas
- Gandharvas – Denizens of heavenly planet who sing very beautifully
- Ganges – The river in India which is sacred and has the ability to wash away the sins. Emanates from Lord Vishnu's toe.

- Garbodakasyayi Vishnu – Expansion of Maha Vishnu which entered each universe.
- Garbodhaka Ocean – Another name of Karana Ocean. Ocean of Reason.
- Ghana – Guard
- Govinda – Refers to Lord Krishna originally. Means cowherd at Gokula
- Halava – A dessert made out of toasted grains, butter and sugar
- Hirangkashipu – The incarnation of Vijaya and the brother of Hirayangkhasha. Obtained a powerful boon from Brahma but was killed by Lord Vishnu as man-lion (Narasimha)
- Hirayangkasha – The incarnation of Jaya as demon. He hid this earthly planet deep inside the cosmic ocean. Killed by Lord Vishnu as boar (Varaha avathar)
- Indra – The king of heavenly kingdoms and the leader of the demigods. Presiding deity of rain and fertility.
- Janaka – Father of Sitadevi and king of Mithila province.
- Janaloka – Heavenly planetary system above Svarga (heaven) populated by sages
- Kailash – Snow capped mountain. Place where where Lord Shiva and his associates resides.
- Kali – Goddess of time, change and destruction. Also associated with empowerment. She is the fierce aspect of Parvathi
- Kamadeva – The god that is responsible to induce lusty desires by shooting his arrow of love.
- Kauravas – The 100 sons of King Dhrtarastra and Gandhahari headed by Duryodhana.
- Khadga – Curved sword

- Khumbakarna – The brother of Ravana. He obtained a boon from Brahma that for 6 months he will sleep and for the next 6 months he will eat continuously
- Kirtika sisters – The sisters who were the initial caretaker of Lord Muruga but is cursed
- Krishna – The eighth incarnation of Lord Vishnu.
- Ksatriya – Members of vedic social order whose occupation is governmental administration and protection of citizens
- Ksirodakasayi Vishnu – The further expansion of Garbodakasyayi Vishnu that entered each and every heart of living beings and the atoms
- Kubera – The treasure of the gods
- Kumaran – Another name of Lord Muruga. Meaning everlasting youth
- Kurukshetra – The battlefield where the great war of Kurukshetra took place 5000 years ago between the Pandavas and Kauravas during the reign of Lord Krishna.
- Kusasthali – City under the sea, constructed by King Revata
- Lakshmana – Brother of Rama. An incarnation of Ananta Sesa
- Lakshmi – Goddess of Fortune and wealth. Wife of Lord Vishnu
- Lankesh – Another name of Ravana. It means Lord of Lanka.
- Lasa – A gentler aspect of Bharatanatyam. Performed by goddess Parvati
- Linga – Anconic symbol of Lord Shiva. Also known as phallus
- Maha Vishnu – The initial form of Lord Vishnu, from which this material creation begins
- Maha-Bhagavata – First class devotee; refers to devotees of Lord Vishnu (the Vaishnavas)

- Mahadeva – Lord Shiva
- Mahadeva – Lord Shiva
- Manas Putras – Mind sons of Lord Brahma totalling to 10 and are the progenitors of the universe.
- Manmadha – Refers to Kamadeva
- Maruts – The storm gods, attendants of Indra
- Modhaka – A white coloured ball filled with paste made from sugar and grated coconut.
- Moksha – Liberation from material bondage. Also known as Mukthi
- Mukthi – Liberation from material bondage
- Muushiga – Mouse of Lord Ganesha
- Naga – Magical snakes. Usually multihooded.
- Nandisvara – The white bull which is the mount of Lord Shiva and also his eternal companion.
- Narada – One of the mind son of Lord Brahma, great sage that always carries veena with him, praising Lord Vishnu.
- Narada – Sage of the gods. A devotee of Lord Vishnu.
- Narasimha – Means man lion. Reafers to 4th incarnation of Lord Vishnu. The purpose is to kill Hirayangkashipu and save Prahlada
- Narayana – Refers to Lord Vishnu. Means 'He who rests on water.
- Netri-kaan – The eye that is situated in the middle of Lord Shiva's forehead.
- Nilakhantha - Means 'Blue throat'. Refers to Lord Shiva as He drank the poison from the Milk Ocean, his throat turns blue.

- Nirguna – Refers to Lord Vishnu or Krishna. Meaning one without material qualities.
- Nyanapanditah – Wisdom Fruit
- Om- the transcendental vibration from everything emanates. A feature of Absolute Truth
- Palkova – A cake like dessert made out of solidified milk
- Pandavas – The five sons of King Pandu and Kuntidevi namely Yudhisthira, Bhimasena, Arjuna, Nakula and Sahadeva.
- Parahamsa – Supreme Swan
- Parashurama – Rama with Axe. The 6th incarnation of Lord Vishnu and is responsible for killing all the kings and emperors around the world 21 times.
- Parvathi – The consort of Lord Shiva. An incarnation of Aadhi Parasakthi.
- Pinaka – The personal bow of Lord Shiva
- Pushpaka Vimana – The chariot which has the ability to change its shape and travel with high speed.
- Raghu – One of the nine planets in Hinduism. Also a snake that is responsible for eclipse of the sun
- Rama – The 7th incarnation of Lord Vishnu. Born to the great King Dasaratha of Ayodya and the protagonist in Ramayana.
- Ramayana – A Hindu epic that narrates the tales of Lord Rama, his exile in the forest and the subsequent battle against Ravana. Written by Valmiki.
- Rasagula – A ball shaped dumplings made from Indian cottage cheese and dough, cooked in light syrup made of sugar
- Ravaita – Son of King Revata; Another name of King Kakudmi

- Ravana – The demon lord who has 10 heads and is terrorizing the universe. He is the historical ruler of the island Lanka which is now the modern day Sri Lanka.
- Revata – Son of King Anarta; descendent of the sun dynasty.
- Rig Veda – The Veda that records hymns to gods, especially to Indra
- Rudraloka – Planet of Lord Shiva
- Sakra – Another name of Indra, means 'the great one'
- Sama veda – The Veda that contains beautiful songs to various gods
- Sara Vana Bhava – Forest of reeds where Lord Skanda first took form as six babies from lava.
- Sarasvathi – Goddess of learning and speech. Lord Brahma's consort
- Shakthi – The incarnation of AadhiSakthi, who was the wife of Lord Shiva. She met her end at her father's sacrificial ceremony. Her death caused Lord Shiva to enter deeply into meditation. Reborn as Parvathi
- Shisupala – Son of King Damaghosa, a very determinant enemy of Lord Krishna. He was killed by Sri Krishna in the Rajasuya sacrifice of King Yudisthira
- Shiva – The god that is in charge of the annihilation of cosmos and the master of this material nature.
- ShivaTandava Stotra – Collection of songs which was composed and sang by Ravana to Lord Shiva
- Siddhi – A mystic yogic perfection
- Sitadevi – The wife of Rama and the daughter of King Janaka of Mithila province.

- Skanda – Another name of Muruga. Meaning beautiful face like flower
- Soma – An intoxicant drink enjoyed by the denizens of heavenly kingdoms
- Sri Hari – Lord Vishnu
- Supersoul – Refers to Ksirodakasyi Vishnu that is in every beings heart
- Surapadman – The demon which terrorized the universe with his powers. He obtained a boon theat he cannot be killed by anyone except Lord Shiva's son. Also known as Tarakasura.
- Svargaloka – The upper planetary systems including the heavenly kingdoms
- Svayamvara – A process whereby a princess selects her husband by garlanding him. Practiced in India thousands of years ago.
- Syamasundara – A name of Lord Krishna. Meaning 'Beautiful blackish boy'
- Tapas – Penance
- Taraksura – Surapadnman
- Thiruvilayadal – Divine sports of Lord Shiva
- Tilaka – Symbol of Lord Vishnu and His devotees. Shaped like an elongated 'U'
- Tretha yuga – Second age of mankind, succeeding Satya yuga and preceeding Dvapara yuga.
- Trimurthi – Trinity of gods who creates, maintains and destroys the universe. Refers to Brahma (creator), Vishnu (preserver) and Shiva (destroyer)
- Trishula – Trident
- Tulasi – One of the dear most devotee of Lord Vishnu or Krishna

- Upanisads – 108 treatises that appear within the Vedas
- Ushas – Dawn personified. They assumed the shape of cows
- Vaanara - Ape
- Vahana – Vehicle.
- Vaikuntha – The abode of Lord Vishnu, located beyond this material jurisdictions
- Vaishnava – Devotees of Lord Vishnu or His incarnations particularly Rama and Krishna
- Vajrayudha – Thunderbolt of Indra
- Vala – Cave where the Ushas were imprisoned
- Varaha – Means boar. Refers to the 3rd incarnation of Lord Vishnu. The purpose is to save this earthly planet which was hid by Hirayangkasha
- Varunadeva – The demigod that is responsible for the affairs pertaining to sea, water and rivers. He is also the god of oath.
- Vayu – Wind god
- Vedantists – Impersonalists who studies the *Vedas*
- Vedas – The books of knowledge namely Rig Veda, Sama Veda, Yajur Veda and Atharva Veda.
- Vedavyasa – The literary incarnation of Godhead
- Veena – A musical instrument with five or more strings
- Vel – Spear of Lord Muruga
- Velava – Another name of Muruga. Means 'One armed with Vel'
- Vibuthi – A symbol of Lord Shiva and his devotees applied on the forehead. It is represented by a streak of line or three lines which is made out of ash.
- Vinayagar – Another name of Lord Ganesha. Means obstacle remover

- Vishnu – The supreme personality of Godhead; the maintainer empowered with full strength, fame, knowledge, beauty, opulence and renunciation
- Vishnu Purana – One of the 18 Mahapurana that elaborates the various avatars of Lord Vishnu and several other stories of the Lord
- Vishvamitra – One of the most venerated sages in Ancient India. Believed to be one of the author of Rig Veda including the Gayatri mantra.
- Visvakarma – Engineer of the gods
- Yakshas – Demoniac attendants of Kubera. Kubera is the King of Yakshas.
- Yama – The god who punishes the sinful people after death.
- Yoga nindram – Meditation while sleeping. Refers to Lord Vishnu's position

REFERENCES

- A.C. Bhaktivedanta Swami Prabhupada. KRSNA- The Supreme Personality of Godhead, Bhaktivedanta Book Trust, 2005, ISBN: 81-89574-18-3.
- A.C. Bhaktivedanta Swami Prabhupada. Bhagavad-Gita As It Is, Bhaktivedanta Book Trust, 2nd edition.
- Songs borrowed and edited from Thiruvilayadal (1965) movie.

ACKNOWLEDGEMENTS

I wish to thank to thank all those who expertise, generously given, has made this book possible.

First and foremost to my uncle; **Sasikumar Krishnan** who patiently helped me through labyrinth of shorts by giving helpful suggestions and information.

To my sister; **Thiveya Vengadasalam** who helped me to prepare the manuscript.

To **Saranyah Jayaraman** who selflessly allowed me to borrow her art to be included in this book.

To **Salaphathy Rao**; my eternal spiritual master who provide me with the knowledge about spirituality.